APOC A LYPSE *noun* 1: a prophetic revelation of the imminent cosmic cataclysm in which God destroys the ruling powers of evil and raises the righteous to life 2: the disclosure of secrets belonging to the last days

The end of the world...

A decade ago, that was a subject reserved for religious fanatics. But now scientists and intellectuals are predicting the demise of civilization as we know it.

In fifteen fact-filled, fast-moving chapters, William R. Goetz demonstrates that the last days may be closer than you think.

APOCALYPSE
NEXT

APOCALYPSE NEXT

by
William R. Goetz

HORIZON HOUSE PUBLISHERS
Beaverlodge, Alberta, Canada

ISBN O-88965-043-8

HORIZON BOOKS
are published by Horizon House Publishers
Box 600, Beaverlodge, Alberta TOH OCO
Printed in the United States of America

Grateful acknowledgment is made to the following publishers for permission to quote from copyrighted material.

Institute in Basic Youth Conflicts, Bill Gothard *Be Alert to Spiritual Danger*, 1980.
Parade Magazine, "Superbugs: A New Biblical Plague?" September 30, 1979
SCP Newsletter, Mark Albrecht, "Welcome to the 1980s," February - March 1980 issue
"Science Speaks" by Peter Stoner. Copyright 1963. *Moody Press*, Moody Bible Institute of Chicago. Used by permission
W.R. Woods News Interests, Wally Wood, Jr. *Cashless Society: A World Without Money*, 1976

To

JOYCE

quiet, gentle, steady, loving

…who has been not only a wonderful

wife and companion for more than

a quarter of a century, but a true

helpmeet, the gracious mother of

our five children and one of God's

best gifts to me.

Contents

Sincere Thanks...

... deep and heartfelt, to:

Danny Spivak, who has immeasurably helped and stimulated me in my study of prophecy through personal encouragement and the kind provision of many books, articles and materials;

the executive board members of my church, for permission to take time from pastoral responsibilities in order to write;

the members of the Sevenoaks Alliance Church "family," who encouraged and prayed for me during my labors on this volume;

Ted and Sunny Cornelson, who graciously allowed the use of their secluded cabin for a number of study, research and writing sessions;

Chris Hopwood, my secretary, who patiently

Sincere Thanks...

... deep and heartfelt, to:

Danny Spivak, who has immeasurably helped and stimulated me in my study of prophecy through personal encouragement and the kind provision of many books, articles and materials;

the executive board members of my church, for permission to take time from pastoral responsibilities in order to write;

the members of the Sevenoaks Alliance Church "family," who encouraged and prayed for me during my labors on this volume;

Ted and Sunny Cornelson, who graciously allowed the use of their secluded cabin for a number of study, research and writing sessions;

Chris Hopwood, my secretary, who patiently

and skillfully deciphered, typed and re-typed the manuscript;

Dr. John Cunningham and Dr. Arnold Cook who reviewed the manuscript; and to Dr. Deane Downey and Milson DeGaris, who edited it grammatically;

and finally, to Neill Foster, friend, evangelist, publisher, without whose gentle persistence there would not have been even the beginning of such an effort on my part.

Prologue

"What *is* going to happen?"

"Will our world perish under a mushroom-shaped nuclear cloud...or are we doomed to the lingering death of a planet that is running out of everything that's vital to our very survival?"

"Is there going to be another war—worse than anything we've ever dreaded or dreamed of in our worst nightmares?"

"What future is there, anyway?"

People are asking questions.

Not always out loud.

But the questions are there—in those quiet times when a pause in activity leaves an unguarded moment for serious thought.

And little wonder...

—when books like *How to Be a Survivor* by the eminent Dr. Paul R. Ehrlich, Professor of Biology at Stanford University, or *Choice of Catastrophe* by Isaac Asimov really "come on strong with the gloom and doom." Asimov writes:

It seems inappropriate...to fear catastrophes to the universe, to the sun, to the earth; we need not dread black holes and extraterrestrial invasion. Instead, we must ask ourselves whether, within the space of this generation, the supply of available energy will finally peak and begin to decline, and whether that will carry down with it human civilization, bring on a desperate last-ditch nuclear war over the waning scraps, and so end all hope of human recovery.[1]

—when daily newscasts indicate that the threat of ruthless Russian aggression, as her military might continues to grow, is increasing;

—when the "doomsday clock" (since 1947 featured on the cover of the *Bulletin of Atomic Scientists* magazine) has its hands moved from nine to seven minutes till midnight, which represents global nuclear war;

—when the world's economic problems seem to mount almost daily; and

—when a conference of 5,000 professional futurists from 40 countries announces in July 1980 in Toronto that planet earth is in deep trouble...[2]

...it's no great surprise to find people desperately concerned over what may be coming—or to find them wondering what to do.

14

Some folks do react strongly to all the doomsday talk. A Religious News Service release dated November 20, 1979, said that

A group of Roman Catholics in Australia are so sure nuclear destruction is imminent they are setting up a retreat in the outback, where they can prepare themselves spiritually for the coming holocaust.

According to reports, some 24 families will form the initial community, to be known as Joseph's Town. They will be joined by several other families as soon as the project gets under way. Supporters plan to build their own church, school, bakery, dairy and clinic.

Meanwhile, another RNS release in September 1979 indicated that

On the banks of the Little Wabash River, not far from Louisville, Illinois, 2,000 people gathered in September 1979 to hear their spiritual leader, Johnny Bob Harrel, teach them how to prepare for the Armageddon he is sure is coming. Classes at the "boot camp for Armageddon" included meat preservation, first aid, weapon loading and, according to the

Associated Press, "how to establish a constitutional money system, preservation of the American family and the Bible's answers to racial questions."

Perhaps you've wondered whether or not *you* should take similar steps to secure, as best you can, a future for yourself and your family. And yet, you may question whether or not the prophets of doom really are right. Perhaps they've totally *misread* the future. After all, *some* futurists, like Herman Kahn, are very optimistic.

This book can help you decide.

Strangely enough, these pages point out that planet earth is, indeed, in for some horrific times ahead. Russia *will* invade Israel. Wars and calamities *are* on the horizon.

The documentation for believing such things will be clearly presented for you to examine and judge...to satisfy yourself as to its validity.

But while none of this sounds particularly encouraging, *this book does hold out a solid hope for each reader.*

Apocalypse Next?

Yes!

But...

YOU CAN BE READY!

PART ONE

Lakes and Lily Pads

A children's riddle given to The Club of Rome—a respected international society of concerned futurists—becomes a parable of the incredible situation that threatens the very survival of the earth and its inhabitants.

17

1

"In the Twenty-Ninth Day— At Evening"

Imagine you own a piece of property on which lies a small lake.

Near the shore is a variety of water lily with a most unusual characteristic: it doubles in size every day. You understand that, if the lily is permitted to grow unchecked, it will completely cover your lake in 30 days, blocking out all light and oxygen, thus choking off every other form of life in the water.

But you're busy—and besides, the lily pad seems small in comparison to the size of the lake. And so for weeks you ignore it, deciding to deal with it when it covers close to half your lake.

On what day will that be?

On the twenty-ninth day, of course. By then you will have only one day left in which to save your lake.

This old French children's riddle was told to the founding meeting of the Club of Rome. The Club is a highly-respected, non-political international body which consists of 100 scientists, educators, economists, political leaders, industrialists and various civil servants. Its members have included Canadian Prime Minister Pierre Elliot Trudeau and several European heads of state. Formed in 1968, it first met in the city of Rome (from which it took its name) to consider a subject of staggering scope—the present and future predicament of the human race. The Club has since met on a regular basis—analyzing earth's problems, seeking solutions, periodically issuing bulletins and reports and attempting to make world leaders recognize the magnitude of our planet's problems so that action can be taken.

In the above riddle, the little lake is our world, and the monstrous lily pad is what the Club of Rome calls the "problematique"—the Global Crisis that has resulted from the fearful increase in population, consumption of resources, industrialization and pollution. They make it quite clear that mankind is in the "evening" of the twenty-ninth day.

The Club points out that these factors have combined to create:

(1) *An incredibly severe drain upon earth's*

raw materials and resources. Knowledgeable leaders project that, at today's rate of consumption, many (if not most) basic commodities will be exhausted by the year 2050;

(2) *The food shortage.* Our planet is already short of food; there is not much unused arable land left, and by 2030 there will be at least twice the present population;

(3) *The energy crisis.* An already serious energy situation has been made worse by recent developments in the Middle East and, after the near disaster at Three Mile Island in 1979, a growing opposition to nuclear energy—which had been hailed as one of mankind's last great energy hopes;

(4) *The pollution problem.* Frightfully little is known about the combined long-term effects of industrial and chemical pollution. Many scientists fear that, with little or no warning, total environmental collapse could come—citing the fact, for example, that if the present ozone and oxygen imbalance gets worse, fearful consequences could result through earth's massive exposure to ultraviolet rays. [3]

But that's not all.

The problems are *synergistic.* That is, all of the difficulties working together make *each* of them more serious than any one of them would be *individually.*

These factors also work *exponentially.* This means that not only does the seriousness of the

21

"problematique" grow rapidly, but the *speed* at which it grows also increases dramatically— just like the lily pad in our lake. It's much like an avalanche rolling down a mountainside... rapidly gathering *both* speed *and* bulk.

TOTAL COLLAPSE PREDICTED

Thus, as earth's population grows, so do the problematic factors that bear upon it and result from it. The Club flatly predicts *the total breakdown and collapse of the world system as we know it by early- to mid-21st century if nothing is done about the problems we now face.* [4] And to make matters worse, to arrive at that conclusion they used and fed into the computer raw statistics only on energy, food, population, and so on—largely ignoring the enormously serious effects of political and social upheaval, including the very real threat of an all-out, global nuclear war.

Is the situation *really* that bad?

After all, through the ages there have always been lots of doomsday prophets. There was considerable apprehension that the world would end as the year 1000 approached. Again, in the twelfth century and in the 1700s, doomsday predictions gained widespread publicity.

In our century, religious groups like the Jehovah's Witnesses and Herbert Armstrong's "Worldwide Church of God" have made various predictions that the present world system would end in 1844, 1914, 1915, 1975...and so on. These, and numerous other endtime cranks and apocalyptic paranoics, have produced lamentable teachings and unbiblical emphases which time has already proven to be wrong.

True! But *now* the most informed and vocal doomsday prophets are the *secular humanists*—the "highest ranking members of this planet's managerial class"—and they appear to have the sheer weight of scientific data and statistics to back them up. The Club has been joined by a veritable chorus of informed voices warning that planet earth and its passenger load are in serious trouble.

Run down a title list of recent books: *How To Be a Survivor, The Terminal Generation, World War III, Future Shock, Armageddon, The Beginning of the End, Approaching the Decade of Shock, Ecospasm, Famine '75, Mankind At the Turning Point*, ad infinitum—many of them written by scientists.

Or look at the cover features of some of our leading and respected news magazines like *Time* or *Newsweek*: "The Energy Crisis"; "Forecast: Earthquake"; "The Age of Disaster"; "To the Brink of Crisis"; "Chemical Catastrophes." Before too long you get the message pretty clearly. Without doubt, informed people are genuinely concerned.

Several quick examples show the gravity of

the situation:

—A car travelling 625 miles uses up as much oxygen as a man breathes in a year; a Boeing 747 burns up 50 tons of oxygen in a single Atlantic crossing. We're told that already sections of the United States produce only 60 percent of the oxygen they consume, and if we go on polluting the oceans, thereby killing the oxygen-producing sea-plants, we could reach the stage where there is no longer enough oxygen to support human life.[5]

—A 1,000 megawatt nuclear power station annually produces 150 gallons of radioactive liquid waste, which must be kept sealed for 2 - 300 years.[6] That's a long time to guarantee against accident...especially after Three Mile Island, Love Canal and the numerous news reports of accidents involving dangerous substances.

—It takes about an acre of fertile, arable land to produce enough food to feed one person on a yearly basis. (The average beer-drinking, heavy meat-eating North American or western European needs the productivity of two acres of such land to support *his* lifestyle!) The amount of land that can be used to grow crops is not unlimited. It is, in fact, severely limited by many factors. Yet, there are now more than four billion people upon earth, all wanting three meals a day. (To put the figure one billion in perspective—consider that an airplane propeller spinning continuously at 2,400 revolu-

24

tions per minute will revolve only 1.26 billion times in a year.) And, according to the projections, in another twenty years there will be an additional three billion mouths to feed—for a total population of over seven billion. [7]

Get the picture?

And remember that these three examples are only small parts of the human problem—merely three isolated perspectives on "the problematique."

Is anything being done?

Not really. There have been some superficial efforts—like banning fluorocarbon aerosols and certain chemical pesticides, promoting efforts to live more simply and urging energy conservation—but mankind's best responses so far have been compared to "giving valium to a terminal cancer patient." Virtually every nation and most individuals are still "looking out for Number One." Consequently, the rich get richer and the poor get poorer—a tragic situation on which *Time* magazine did an in-depth feature report several years ago entitled "Poor vs. Rich: A New Global Conflict."

THE CLUB PROPOSALS

Thus *The Limits to Growth*, the first Club of Rome report, issued in 1972, warned that if a cooperative global effort to deal with the "problematique" was not well underway by 1980, the situation would be severe, if not irreversible. The Club made the following proposals, which by and large have not been acted upon:

1. Survival of this planet necessitates "new forms of thinking that will lead to a fundamental revision of human behavior and, by implication, of the entire fabric of present-day society."

2. Population growth must be checked and redistributed.

3. Developed nations *must not* maintain their superior status, but wealth and technology will have to be redistributed in a global Robin Hood effort.

4. This generation will have to make substantial material sacrifices for future generations.

5. The world should be divided into ten regions which would be economically interdependent. Furthermore, the redress of the "problematique" must be the Number One priority of each individual and nation.

6. All this would be "guided by a rational master plan." Needless to say, this proposal amounts to a One World Government with the resources to produce such a plan and the power to enforce it. National chauvinism would be a thing of the past. [8]

Almost everyone who has looked objectively at the problems we face comes to the same conclusion: If global unity in confronting these problems is not achieved, THERE WILL BE TOTAL COLLAPSE. It is not a matter of *whether*, but *when*.

The chance of such global unity being achieved (demanding as it does a radical change in human nature) is almost zero. Indeed, as the Club report laments, "Mankind has made virtually no new discoveries to increase the rate of social change."

THE SITUATION IS SERIOUS

All this serves to underscore the seriousness of our situation. *And nothing is being done!* The Club's report says that "only a small fraction of the world's population is actively concerned with understanding these problems or seeking their solutions." One scientist, with grim humor, used this metaphor:

> We are aboard a train which is gathering speed, racing down a track on which there is an unknown number of switches leading to unknown destinations. No single scientist is in the engine cab, and there may be demons at the switch. Most of society is in the caboose— looking backward. [9]

Another author says the state of humanity reminds him of a runaway train headed downhill with the engine jammed wide open—it being only a matter of time till civilization's "train" is derailed.

The President of the Club of Rome, Aurelio Peccei, was interviewed by the Paris magazine *Vision* late in 1978 on the tenth anniversary of the founding of the Club. In the interview he said he found mankind "more confused, more worried, less secure than ten years ago."

When the interviewer said, "You sound pessimistic about the future," Peccei replied,

> We issued a warning ten years ago, but looking back we feel it was so easy to do something *then*—and so difficult *now*. We think that mankind has perhaps only ten years or less to choose a course different from the present one—which is bound to end in disaster. [10]

And then there's The Bomb.

Strangely enough, two of mankind's most fearful problems—the nuclear threat and the innate human selfishness that makes war almost inevitable—have been given little attention by the Club of Rome. But they are frightful factors that have the capacity to bring about the demise of civilization as we know it.

For example, the 1979 SALT II (Strategic

Arms Limitation Talks) agreement between the U.S. and the U.S.S.R.—before the Soviet invasion of Afghanistan in December 1979 caused the agreement to be rejected by the U.S. Senate—was made when the U.S. had 2,060 Strategic Nuclear Delivery Systems, the most advanced of which is the Minuteman III, armed with three MIRVs (acronym for "multiple independently targetable re-entry vehicles") capable of delivering a 1,005 kiloton force—more than fifty times the force of the Hiroshima A-bomb. But the Soviets at the same time had 2,570 Nuclear Delivery Systems in their arsenal—the most advanced of which is the SS-18, an incredibly powerful intercontinental ballistic missile (ICBM) armed with ten MIRVs *each* capable of delivering a 1,000 kiloton force: in other words, a total force over five hundred times the power of the Hiroshima bomb! [11]

It's been calculated that in early 1980 the total megatonnage lying about in ICBM silos and bomb racks equalled 1.3 million Hiroshima infernos! And yet, incredibly, still more are being built to "balance" the nuclear armament stockpiles of Russia and the U.S.A. All of this is to say nothing of the conventional armed forces of just the two superpowers alone—uniformed armies of nearly 6.5 million between them, with thousands of tactical aircraft, tanks, field artillery, warships and submarines.

Nor are the two superpowers alone in the

nuclear "club." According to the U.S. Joint Committee on Atomic Energy, there were six nations with nuclear capacity at the end of 1979. By 1983 another nine nations are expected to have joined their ranks, eleven more by 1986, and by 1990 a total of 35 nations are expected to have the capacity to destroy the world with nuclear weaponry. [12]

Equally as frightening as this is the specter of germ warfare. Indications are that both the U.S. and Russia are working on bacteriological and chemical warfare techniques. Early 1980 newspaper reports, denied by the Soviets, charged that in April 1979 a large number of people in the major Russian industrial center of Sverdlovsk were contaminated and died as a result of an accident involving a "lethal biological agent."

The January 1980 issue of *The Intelligence Digest*, Cheltenham, Gloucestershire, England, indicated:

> Unconfirmed reports from Afghan guerrillas state that Soviet forces have already used limited chemical warfare against the *mujahdin*. Use of Soviet nerve and other toxic gases against Meo tribesmen in Laos and against Cambodian guerrillas by North Vietnamese forces has been confirmed by interviews with survivors, so there is little doubt that Soviet

Army units in Afghanistan will employ chemical warfare against the rebels...U.S. intelligence has already confirmed the presence of Soviet Army chemical warfare units inside Afghanistan. Of great potential danger to the nearly one million Afghan refugees in Pakistan and Iran is the arsenal of Soviet biological weapons. By use of various delivery means, "germ warfare" of a long-range strategic nature can be used against densely-packed refugee camps inside Pakistan and Iran to cause lingering death and disease. To trace such germ warfare to the Soviets will be very difficult due to the nature of the illnesses. Soviet biological warfare against Afghan rebel sanctuaries is a distinct possibility and will be extremely difficult to authenticate. [13]

To put all of these recent developments into perspective, it is deeply disturbing to realize that in 55 centuries of recorded history there have only been 292 years of "peace" (that is, years in which there was no war raging somewhere on earth). Furthermore, mankind has never yet fashioned a weapon that hasn't been used. Indeed, both nuclear and chemical weapons have already been used in warfare, and many observers believe they'll be used again.

Thus, humanity's penchant for using whatever weapons it can create—however horrible the consequences—coupled with the moral shortcomings and innate selfishness of the human race, simply adds immeasurably to the grim outlook for earth's future. Many believe that the terrifying prospect of our planet vanishing in a nuclear super-holocaust is all too possible.

When the two variables above are taken into account, along with the Club's scientific computer findings (which are already going off the charts), it appears that the virtual collapse of the world system as we know it is indeed unavoidable.

Little wonder that the world *despairs*— expressed in songs like David Bowie's *Five Years*.

Pushing through the market square, so
    many mothers sighing,
News had just come over, we had five
    years left to cry in.
News guy wept when he told us, earth was
    really dying—
Cried so much his face was wet, then I
    knew he was not lying...
We got five years, my brain hurts a lot.
We got five years, that's all we got.

Or people attempt to cope with earth's horrifying prospects through *escapism* into "The Good Old Days" or "Happy Days," by *radical idealism*, by *self-indulgence* ("Eat, drink and be merry—for tomorrow we die"), or by a *wishful optimism* which ignores the facts.

WHAT ARE THE OPTIONS?

According to the Club of Rome, there aren't many, nor are they any too attractive. Here are the most likely:

1. Industrial growth and consumption will deplete the resource base of the planet. This, combined with rapid population increase, will lead to a total collapse in energy availability, the economy, food production and, inevitably, political and social structures. Famine, disease and lack of heat in winter will kill most of the population in a short time.

2. Total or near total environmental collapse will occur. Again, most of the population will die, for the planet will not support basic forms of plant life and the food chain will be broken.

3. A nuclear war will wipe out most of the people in the northern hemisphere.

4. Humanity will realize the full impact of the predicament in ten to twenty years and make a last-ditch cooperative effort to unite under a single government or ruler. But it will be too little too late, and will only forestall the inevitable collapse. [14]

In any of the above four options it would be possible for earth to survive and eventually replenish itself to some degree. If 90 percent of the population died, the earth would be thrown back to the population count of about 1,000 years ago. However, resource depletion would likely prevent the rise of another civilization as large and diverse as this one.

What *is* clear is that the human race has never before faced the situation that it does today. The present crisis is literally unimaginable for most people. Its massive and seemingly irreversible proportions make it highly unlikely that this is a passing perturbation. It cannot be considered a socio-economic "phase" that the earth is going through and will recover from in another 50 years. All the talk of the dawning of an Age of Aquarius, the "Age of Enlightenment" and the advent of a glorious "New Age" of love and cosmic consciousness is unmitigated nonsense. Such a hope, however well-intended, cuts totally against the grain of reality. Life on this sad sphere is getting radically *worse*, not better.

THERE'S ANOTHER POSSIBILITY

But there's another very real option, not considered by the Club of Rome.

It's a possibility which a group of ancient prophets—who have had an amazing record of accuracy (would you believe 100 percent?) — have outlined in great detail.

That possibility is that Jesus Christ will return to deal with the insurmountable problems facing this globe—and to establish His Kingdom here upon planet earth.

I firmly believe this to be more than just a possibility. I am convinced that this option outlines THE WAY IT ACTUALLY WILL BE for a world presently reeling under unimaginable pressures and problems. I invite you to consider with me this fifth option in the pages of this book. It's a consideration which could literally save your life!

But before we get into that, let's pause briefly to look, in Part Two, at that amazing group of prophets whom we've already mentioned. Let's consider the prophets themselves, their backgrounds and the ground rules covering their prophecies. We need to check out their validity and their right to even be given a serious hearing.

After all, it really does look as if we're in "the evening of the twenty-ninth day." Time is running out, and we just don't have ages in which to be led down the garden path to the wrong solutions!

PART TWO

Prophets and Prophecies

A group of ancient Hebrew prophets [with a record to date of 100 percent accuracy] had a great deal to say about a solution to earth's massive problems. Their detailed prophetic utterances were made under very stringent conditions. We need to check them out.

2

Psychics—or Prophets?

It created something of a stir in the small city where I was living. A clairvoyant had come to town and the area's "second" newspaper, struggling to get going and grasping at straws, did a two-page feature article on her— undoubtedly in the vain hope that it could build circulation through sensationalism. Whatever the reason, the story generated a lot of interest.

Understandably, the future is big business these days. It seems everybody wants to know what's going to happen, particularly in view of the world situation as we've just looked at it.

Predictions by past and present clairvoyants like Jeane Dixon, Edgar Cayce and Frances Drake are eagerly read by multitudes.

Hot line radio and TV shows thrive on the psychics.

The makers of horoscopes do a rousing business—in the newspapers, magazines and book stores. Even little towns and villages have their own tea cup readers and small time

39

clairvoyants.

Books on prophecy sell extremely well.

Others turn to the darker side of "the hidden"—to tarot cards, magic and the occult—in an effort to draw aside the curtain that veils the future. The ancient rites of witchcraft are once again seriously practiced in many parts of the world—including North America.

Certainly there's no shortage of twentieth century seers—most of whom expect to be paid for their efforts. But there's a vast difference between a seer and a bona fide prophet.

Present-day seers have a long—though not a very noble—heritage. Dating back to biblical times, their forerunners were the magicians, astrologers, sorcerers, witches and Chaldeans. Magicians were the special, sacred scribes. Astrologers and witches were the conjurers— those who cast spells through the spirit medium. Sorcerers engaged in the black magic arts, and the Chaldeans were the priest caste of them all.

Though much of what ancient and modern seers did, and continue to do, is phoney, yet there is also undoubtedly real, though evil, power in at least some of their practices.

THEY TEND TO MISS A LOT

Particularly today, however, the seers and

clairvoyants, the psychics and astrologers, are most often totally wrong in their predictions. For example, numerous publications carry every New Year's the predictions of various psychics for the coming year. Anyone who bothers to keep a box score on such forecasts soon discovers that the rate of inaccuracy is extremely high.

According to a Religious News Service report in January 1980, psychic-astrologer Frederick Davis predicted that in 1979 Pope John Paul II would "stagger the religious world by announcing his plans for the ordination of women priests." (It hasn't happened yet!)

Other totally inaccurate predictions from the psychic fantasies of 1979 included these:

> "Blood will be spilled as fighting breaks out between Israel and Egypt again in May. Surprisingly, [CBS anchorman] Walter Cronkite will be influential in getting both sides back to the conference table, where a new peace agreement will be hammered out." (There was *no* Israeli-Egyptian fighting in 1979; instead, moves toward normal relations began.)

> "Muhammad Ali will win a seat in Congress." (Instead, in early 1980, he won an assignment from Carter in Africa.)

> "President Carter will be injured in a hang-gliding accident between April 9 and 10." (Nothing of the sort occurred.)

> "Uganda dictator Idi Amin will be assassinated March 13, 1979." (He was still alive in September 1980.)

These and other predictions relating to an "alien space station," the stopping of inflation "dead in its tracks," and so on, were published in editions of the *National Enquirer* and *The Star*—the supermarket staples.

In 1979 predictions, neither Jeane Dixon nor any of the ten leading psychics had a word to say about Iran, let alone predicting the upheaval there and the taking of American hostages.

Jeane Dixon, perhaps one of the best known of the psychics—whose book *A Gift of Prophecy* was condensed in *Reader's Digest* (bringing her instant fame, particularly because she apparently "foresaw" President Kennedy's assassination)—has an appallingly low "success rate" of less than 40 percent accuracy.

Among other things, she predicted war with China in the 1970s, President Carter's stepping down, and a number of other major inaccuracies involving well-known persons—like the late Pope John Paul, whom she said, in 1977, would be around for four more years. [15]

Jeane Dixon would not last long on the basis of the ground rules under which the true prophets operated.

Those ancient Hebrew prophets, who have given us the detailed prophecies which we will shortly consider, were men who had to be willing to stake their very lives on the absolute truth of their prophetic messages.

Here's how.

THE ACID TEST

Israel's great deliverer and leader, Moses, writing in the Pentateuch, said that through the course of the nation's history many prophets would come to declare God's Word to the Jewish people. Moses was asked at that point how the nation could "know the word which God has not spoken." His answer, recorded in Deuteronomy 18:22, was simple, and is the acid test of a true prophet: "When a prophet speaks in the name of the Lord, if the word does not come to pass, that is a word which the Lord has not spoken."

And the penalty, under Jewish law, for *falsely* claiming to be a prophet was *death*. Capital punishment by stoning.

Even under such harsh conditions, however, many of the prophets made *short-term prophecies*, which could be, and were, fulfilled in *their* lifetimes. Obviously, they were for real.

Others gave long-range prophecies, or prophecies which undoubtedly had a double reference, that is, both a short- *and* a long-term meaning. Many of such prophecies, especially prophecies about the Messiah, have *short-term references*—to Christ's first appearance on earth (already fulfilled and documented by history)—as well as *long-term references*—to His second coming.

Frequently, the prophets did not themselves understand the significance of their own utterances, as the Apostle Peter points out in his New Testament book II Peter.

Of course, to be valid, a prophecy must be of such a nature that the one who utters it cannot influence its fulfillment—prevented either by time or circumstances from interfering in its outcome.

It must also be in sufficient detail that it can't have numerous possible meanings, so that the prophet cannot cop out.

THOSE ANCIENTS MEASURE UP

The Hebrew prophets, whose utterances (given as long as 3-4,000 years ago) have been preserved for us in the Bible, clearly meet all of these criteria.

In fact, *all* of the short- and many of the long-term prophecies (all those due for fulfillment) have actually come to pass.

For example, Isaiah prophesied over a span of about 60 years during the reign of four successive kings of Judah. His authenticity as a bona fide spokesman for God, when submitted to Moses' acid test, was demonstrated time and again.

During the reign of Hezekiah about 710 B.C., the mighty Assyrian army led by the cruel King Sennacherib invaded and besieged Jerusalem. As recorded in Isaiah 36:36-38, the prophet made a short-term prophecy that, contrary to Sennacherib's plans and threats, he would not attack Jerusalem. Instead, he would return to his own land.

History records that's how it happened. When a rumor of internal problems at home reached Sennacherib, he abandoned the siege, returned home and was assassinated—with his own sons doing the dastardly deed!

Isaiah also made long-range predictions.

In chapter 39:5-7, he predicted that Babylon would destroy Judah and carry away all the treasures of Israel...with the surviving sons of royalty becoming eunuchs at Babylon. *Just over 100 years later*, in 586 B.C., this prediction came to pass.

Then, as recorded in Isaiah 13:17-22, the prophet foretold that the invincible Babylonian Empire would be conquered and the city of Babylon so completely destroyed that it would be uninhabitable. That prophecy meant really going out on a limb, for at the time it was uttered Babylon was considered to be an impregnable city with walls 150 feet high and so thick that five chariots abreast could drive on top of them. The city, one of the seven wonders of the ancient world, was also so self-sustaining that it was thought to be impervious to siege.

But approximately *150 years* after Isaiah prophesied, on October 16, 539 B.C., Babylon fell to the Medes and Persians. Ultimately, the city sank into ruin from which it has never recovered...though Iraq is currently attempting to reconstruct that ancient city.

Again Isaiah prophesied that a king whom he actually named—Cyrus—would make possible the rebuilding of the Temple and Jerusalem by allowing any Jewish captives who wished to do so to return to Palestine for this work. The prophecy is recorded in Isaiah 44:28 to 45:4. *Two hundred years* later the Persian King Cyrus granted Jewish exiles, remaining from the Babylonian captivity, to return to Jerusalem for the work of reconstruction, even providing requisitions for materials!

It's quite an impressive record for Isaiah—*if* he was just guessing. A most unlikely short-term prophecy...right on; then three completely accurate long-term forecasts of 100, 150 and 200 years. And these are only four of numerous prophetic utterances by the major Old Testament prophets. Only divine revelation can explain such feats of foresight.

Some scholars who would like to explain away the miracle of prophecy have charged that Isaiah lived later in history than claimed. Their "late dating" of Isaiah implies that he wrote his so-called prophecies after they actually happened, making him a fraud.

But such a charge makes more than Isaiah a fraud. It also makes the Jewish people, who have retained for posterity Isaiah's writings and whose Museum of the Scroll in Jerusalem houses the Isaiah manuscripts found in the 1940s, deceivers and charlatans, to say nothing of its violation of the consistent witness of history.

Obviously Isaiah was for real.

SO WAS EZEKIEL

Consider one other example.

Both Isaiah and the prophet Ezekiel prophesied the destruction of the powerful commercial center of Tyre. Ezekiel added the intriguing details that the walls and towers of Tyre would be broken, the very dust scraped from her site and that site made like the top of a rock—a place for the spreading of nets (Ezekiel 26:4-5).

At the time of the prediction (588 B.C.) it must have seemed absurd, for Tyre was then indeed a strong city-state. In fact, so well-fortified was the city that for thirteen years (from 585-573 B.C.) it withstood Nebuchadnezzar's attempts to overthrow it. Nebuchadnezzar succeeded only in destroying the mainland fortress, but the island city of Tyre—just a short distance off-shore—remained free and the excellent Phoenician sailors inhabiting it continued their commerce.

But in 332 B.C., Alexander the Great, determined to take Tyre, constructed a causeway out to it, in the process literally scraping the soil from the site of the city down to the bare rock. Thus mainland Tyre was so devastated that the ancient site can scarcely be identified. Fishermen now spread their nets on the rock where once it stood!

Daniel, Jeremiah, Ezekiel, Micaiah, David, Micah...on and on the list could go...prophets who passed the test. Their prophetic utterances came to pass. To be fair, we must acknowledge that there are those who dispute the claim of inerrancy for the prophets. But such positions are invariably taken when the "law of double reference" is ignored.

Concerning the birth, life, death and resurrection of Jesus Christ, over 60 prophetic utterances by more than a dozen different prophets were literally fulfilled—though given, in some cases, as much as 1,000 years previous to His birth.

Josh McDowell, in *Evidence that Demands a Verdict*, points out that Peter Stoner (*Science*

Speaks, Moody Press, 1963) demonstrates that the possibility of *coincidence* in the fulfillment of the 60 specific prophecies through Christ's birth, life, death and resurrection is *ruled out* by the science of probability. Stoner says that by using the modern science of probability in reference to *just eight* of these,

we find that the chance that any man might have lived down to the present time and fulfilled all eight prophecies is 1 in 10^{17}. That would be 1 in 100,000,000,000,000,000. In order to help us comprehend this staggering probability, Stoner illustrates it by supposing that we take 10^{17} silver dollars and lay them on the face of Texas. They will cover all of the state to a depth of two feet. Now mark one of these silver dollars and stir the whole mass thoroughly, all over the state. Blindfold a man and tell him that he can travel as far as he wishes, but he must pick up one silver dollar and say that this is the right one. What chance would he have of getting the right one? Just the same chance that the prophets would have had of writing these eight prophecies and having them all come true in any one man, from their day to the present time, providing they wrote them in their own wisdom.... Now these prophecies were either given by inspiration of God or the prophets just wrote them as they thought they should be. In such a case the prophets had just one chance in 10^{17} of having them come true in any man, but they all came true in Christ.

This means that the fulfillment of these eight prophecies alone proves that God inspired the writing of those prophecies to a definiteness which lacks only one chance in 10^{17} of being absolute.

Stoner considers 48 prophecies and says, "We find the chance that any one man fulfilled all 48 prophecies to be 1 in 10^{157}." [16]

To visualize a number so large is a virtual impossibility. And remember, it was not just 8, or 48, but 60 prophecies which Jesus completely and totally fulfilled, demonstrating that prophecy completed in Jesus Christ is a powerful testimony to both *His* and the *prophets'* authenticity.

These are historical facts that cannot be successfully disputed. Sir Robert Anderson of Scotland Yard spent many years of his life verifying and validating the details of Daniel's prophecy. Anderson's book, *The Coming Prince*, published in 1890, clearly underscores the fact that Daniel gave not only specific years but a sequence for future major events, the accuracy of which cannot be denied.

Obviously, these men were not mere *seers* or *psychics*—with a record of partial accuracy. They were *prophets*, whose utterances have been vindicated as being from God because all their prophecies whose time for fulfillment has already come *have been literally fulfilled* with 100 percent accuracy.

Their noble ranks include even Jesus Christ—the greatest of all Prophets, for He uttered many specific prophecies—and the apostles, like Peter, Paul and John of Patmos, whose Revelation is the final book of the sacred canon.

And so the word of these men, in terms of prophecies still to be fulfilled, may be *completely depended upon*. Their utterances have the stamp of divine authenticity upon them. While much of what they said is still future, it is apparent that we are beginning to see fulfillment of many of their predictions...in our time.

Now—in the next chapter—we'll sketch an overview of these yet-to-be-fulfilled prophecies. They point to the one solution to our planet's problems that, unfortunately, has been missed by earth's troubled, perplexed leaders.

For further reading:
The Late Great Planet Earth (pp 9-31) by Hal Lindsey

Evidence That Demands a Verdict by Josh McDowell

More Evidence That Demands a Verdict by Josh McDowell

More Than a Carpenter by Josh McDowell

"Prophecy is merely history
written in advance."

"History is *His* story."

3

History in Advance—and its Focus

We were on an Air Canada flight out of
Vancouver, B.C., and the topic turned to
prophecy. After about an hour of conversation,
my seatmate—a computer technician with
whom I had just gotten acquainted—said,
"O.K. So what's going to be the scenario from
here on out?"

A good question.

The answer is one on which not even all
students of prophecy fully agree.* However, the
overview I gave that technician, and which I
want to share with you in this chapter, is one
which I am obviously convinced is a biblically
sound, sane, accurate interpretation of the

---

* For those who are theologically inclined:

There are three major views among students of
prophecy concerning the end times.

One view holds that the return of Jesus Christ to earth

53

many utterances of those authentic prophets discussed in the previous chapter.

I am convinced of the accuracy of this overview after years of study. While I am not dogmatic about every little detail (I don't think anybody can be), I believe the major outline unquestionably to be the message of the prophets. It is a view adopted by a majority of prophetic students today.

So—putting together *all* of the messages of the prophets who prophesied over a period of more than 1,000 years—what do we foresee?

IMAGINE SOME MOUNTAIN RANGES

Perhaps the best way to visualize the future would be to imagine a series of mountain ranges stretching out to the horizon—with each range

---

will not occur until after the prophesied period of 1,000 years of peace, called the Millennium.

Another holds that there will be no Millennium—equating it with the church age.

The third view is that the return of Christ precedes, and in fact, precipitates the Millennium. This school believes that the Rapture and the Tribulation both precede the Millennium, with the Rapture occurring either before, during, or at the end of the Tribulation, depending upon the viewpoint held.

The author holds the Pre-Tribulation, Pre-Millennial view.

or peak representing a prophetic high point.
Think of the prophets themselves as standing at
various vantage points in relationship to these
ranges—some farther off, some closer, others
actually within the nearer mountains—looking
upon this series of "prophetic peaks" and
describing what they see (see Fig. 1, p. 65).

Just before we point out the prophet's view of
the "peaks," let me explain that we're not
going to stop to document each statement or
prophecy as we go along. Rather, each one will
be footnoted with the reference(s) in the Bible
where it can be located and verified.

And this needs to be said about the
Bible—the world's all-time best-seller. It claims
to be the Word of God and, in spite of many
vicious attacks upon it over the centuries, it
gives every evidence to the intellectually honest
seeker of being just what it claims to be. To
present the evidence for the authenticity and
authorship of the Bible is beyond the scope of
this book. Besides, it has already been done by
many scholars far more able than this writer.
So, take it as solid documentation—in perfect
confidence. And don't, please, just accept my
word on the prophetic viewpoints presented
here. Find a Bible and check them out.

One further word. Don't turn me off when I
write about what may seem to be matters little
related to our current global crises. Stick with
me and you'll see clearly how it all fits together.

So finally, we come to our overview of "prophecy's peaks." As we do so, we must realize that, from our vantage point in time, we now have to look *back* on some of these. For us they have already become history. But remember: at the time they were uttered, they were all prophecy...or "history written in advance."

The first peak we note is the prophecy that the twelve-tribe nation of Israel would be divided into two nations—ten northern tribes and two southern tribes. The northern tribes would be conquered first and carried away into a captivity from which they would not return for centuries.

The southern tribes would also be conquered but, though carried off into 70-year captive exile, would return and remain in their land of Palestine. [a]

The second peak, a very major one, concerns the coming of the Messiah—the Lord Jesus Christ. His birth, life, death, resurrection and ascension were prophesied in great detail. [b]

The third highpoint is the descent of the Holy Spirit to earth—following the ascension to heaven of Jesus Christ—to usher in what has been called the "age of the Church." (The Church, in the Bible, is that group of people from all eras, and from all around the world, who have come into a personal relationship by faith in Jesus Christ—the Lord and Head of the church. More on this later.) [c]

The fourth prophetic peak has to do with the two tribes of Israel still remaining, at the time of Christ, in Palestine. The prophecy was that they would be cruelly and completely rooted out of their land and dispersed among all the nations of the earth. At the same time, their temple would be utterly destroyed and Jerusalem would become a Gentile (that is, a non-Jewish) city until "the times of the Gentiles are at an end." [d]

The rise and fall of various world powers are seen as the next series of ranges. [e]

Then, somewhat removed in time from the prophecies we have already looked at, we see, as a part of a rather closely connected range, a whole series of events: the people of Israel begin to return to the land of Palestine and become a nation once again; [f] a nation to the north of Israel becomes a great power in the earth; [g] a military power from the east develops the capacity to field an incredible force of soldiers—200 million; [h] one of the ancient world powers, described earlier by the prophets, is revived in a ten-nation confederacy; [i] the Arab nations (sons of Ishmael in Scripture) become a global factor; [j] and enormous problems, coupled with loss of faith and an occult explosion, come upon the earth. [k]

I scarcely need to point out here that all of these prophecies mentioned to this point are

57

either already history or are in the process of being fulfilled.

So now we get to the specific question my companion asked me on that Air Canada flight: "What's the scenario from here on out?" The remaining peaks in our visualized prophetic ranges spell it out.

THE REMAINING PROPHETIC PEAKS

The next event is the instantaneous disappearance of perhaps millions of people from the earth—in what has come to be called the Rapture. This is the sudden catching away, by the Lord Jesus Christ, of the Church—all those who are personally related by faith to Him. [l]

Then will follow a great number of virtually simultaneous events—crowded into a period of about seven years.

Russia and her allies invade Israel—and are supernaturally defeated in one of earth's major, but short-lived, military actions. [m]

A ruler who quickly becomes a global power arises out of the ten-nation confederacy, makes a seven-year treaty with Israel, aids in the reconstruction of the temple in Jerusalem, but halfway through the treaty demands to be worshipped there as God. The result is a complete turnabout from his treaty with Israel and a dreadful persecution of the Jews by him. [n]

During all of this period, catastrophic judgments from God are being poured out upon the world—which, with the removal of the Church, has become unbelievably godless. [o]

This seven-year period culminates with the war of Armageddon—when the armies of the world ruler called the Antichrist, with the Arab confederacy, a 200 million man force from the Far East and the remnant of the Russian power bloc, converge on Palestine. [p]

At that point, Jesus Christ and the armies of heaven appear, and the Lord of Glory defeats the entire massed armies of earth. [q] Jesus Christ will then personally establish a thousand-year reign of righteousness, peace, justice and prosperity upon the earth. [r]

At the conclusion of this period, called the Millennium, there will be—incredibly—a final rebellion by man against God. It will be put down and, following God's righteous judgment of all, the old earth will be purged with fire, a new heavens and earth will take its place and eternity will be ushered in. [s]

You say, "Wow! All these things sound incredible! I can hardly believe them!"

Remember—they've all been prophesied. And to date those prophets have a 100 percent accurate batting average.

In the next section of this book, we'll take a sane, carefully reasoned look at world events now in progress, or on the horizon, that lead

many people to believe the final fulfillment of
the vision of the prophets is upon us.

THE FOCUS OF ALL PROPHECY

Just before we do that, however, we need to
understand what is the focus not only of all
prophecy, but of all Scripture.

That focus is a Person: The Lord Jesus
Christ—the Son of God.

It has been said that history is His story. He
divides all of time into two periods:
B.C.—Before Christ, and A.D.—Anno
Domini...in the year of our Lord.

When He came to earth, taking upon Himself
human form, in order to live a sinless life and
then to die upon the cross, He won the victory of
the ages. A sentence of ultimate defeat and
doom was passed upon Satan and the forces of
evil because of Christ's death and resurrection.
That sentence has not yet been *executed*, but it
will be. Both Jesus Christ Himself and many of
the prophets have promised it. He is victor, and
His ultimate triumph is sure.

In that hour, every knee shall bow—of things
in heaven, and on earth and under the
earth—and every tongue will admit that Jesus
Christ is Lord, to the glory of God the Father.

Yes! *He* is the focus of prophecy...of history
and of all time. His coming in glorious power
will set earth right. That is apparent just from

the brief overview we've taken, and will be more fully spelled out in Parts Three and Five.

Do you personally know Him?

You can, and you need to.

You see, Jesus Christ also divides all mankind into two groups. It's impossible to be neutral about Him. Either you agree with His claims and *accept* Him for whom and what He says He is, or you *reject* Him. He Himself said, "He who is not *for* me is *against* me."

ONLY FOUR OPTIONS ABOUT CHRIST

There are only four possible conclusions a thinking person can come to concerning Jesus Christ. He's either a *liar*, a *lunatic*, a *legend* or He is *Lord*! In the light of the claims He made about Himself and the things the prophets said of Him, He has to be one of these four.

Consider: if He knew the claims He made were not true, but He made them anyway—then, of course, He was a liar.

If He believed His claims, but they weren't true, then He was deluded. And in view of the nature of these claims, nothing short of a lunatic.

If He didn't make the claims attributed to Him—but they were simply the work of an enthusiastic (but misguided) band of followers—then He is merely a legend.

But for a person to accept *any one* of these

three options about Christ, however sincerely or sympathetically, is to reject Him and to be against Him.

The truth is that *history* gives the lie to each of these "options" about Jesus Christ. The only logical conclusion a thinking person can come to is that He is who He claimed to be.

He and He alone is worthy to be Lord!

Don't lose sight of that fact as we now explore the indications that lead us to believe that Jesus Christ, the focus of prophecy, is soon to return.

For Further Reading:
Evidence That Demands a Verdict by Josh McDowell

The following selected Scripture portions are not intended to be an exhaustive list of the evidence which could be marshalled in support of the statements which they footnote. Any reader who wishes to make a detailed study of the biblical prophetic texts is directed to the **Salem Kirban Reference Bible.**

(a) Deuteronomy 28:1-60; Isaiah 18:2; Jeremiah 9:13-16; 15:4; 18:16,17; Ezekiel 12:15,20; 22:5; Hosea 8:8; 9:17; and Amos 9:8,9

(b) Old Testament PROPHECY	New Testament FULFILLMENT
Gen. 3:15	Gal. 4:4
Gen. 18:18	Acts 3:25

(b) Old Testament PROPHECY	New Testament FULFILLMENT
Gen. 17:19	Matt. 1:2
Num. 24:17	Lk. 3:34
Gen. 49:10	Lk. 3:33
Isa. 9:6,7	Matt. 1:1
Micah 5:2	Matt. 2:1
Dan. 9:25	Lk. 2:1,2
Isa. 7:14	Matt. 1:18
Jer. 31:15	Matt. 2:16
Hosea 11:1	Matt. 2:14
Isa. 9:1,2	Matt. 4:12-16
Deut. 18:15	John 6:14
Psa. 110:4	Heb. 6:20
Isa. 53:3	John 1:11
Isa. 11:2	Lk. 2:52
Zech. 9:9	John 12:13,14
Psa. 41:9	Mark 14:10
Zech. 11:12	Matt. 26:15
Zech. 11:13	Matt. 27:6,7
Psa. 109:7,8	Acts 1:18-20
Psa. 27:12	Matt. 26:60,61
Isa. 53:7	Matt. 26:62,63
Isa. 50:6	Mark 14:65
Psa. 69:4	John 15:23-35
Isa. 53:4,5	Matt. 8:16,17
Isa. 53:12	Matt. 27:38
Psa. 22:16	John 20:27
Psa. 22:6-8	Matt. 27:39,40
Psa. 69:21	John 19:29
Psa. 22:8	Matt. 27:43
Psa. 109:4	Lk. 23:34
Zech. 12:10	John 19:34
Psa. 22:18	Mark 15:24
Psa. 34:20	John 19:33
Isa. 53:9	Matt. 27:57-60
Psa. 16:10	Matt. 28:9
Psa. 68:18	Lk. 24:50,51

(c) Isaiah 32:15; 59:12; Ezekiel 39:29; Joel 2:28; Zech. 12:10

(d) Luke 21:24

(e) Daniel chapters 2 and 7

(f) Isaiah 11:11; Jeremiah 30:3; 36:37; Ezekiel 11:17; 20:34; 36:8-11; 37:1-10,16-22; Zechariah 10:10

(g) Ezekiel chapter 38 (note vs. 15)

(h) Revelation 9:16; 16:12

(i) Daniel 2:41-45; 7:19-28

(j) Genesis 16:10,12; 17:20

(k) Matthew 24:4-8,23,24,32-42; Luke 21:25-33; II Timothy 3:1-9

(l) I Corinthians 15:51-58; I Thessalonians 4:14-18; Titus 2:13

(m) Ezekiel chapters 38 and 39. Note that the Russian invasion could possibly precede the Rapture.

(n) Ezekiel 38:8; Daniel 7:24; 8:25; 9:27; 11:40; Revelation chapter 6

(o) Revelation 6:2-17; 8:1-9:21; 11:15; 16:2-21

(p) Joel 3:2,12-14; Revelation 16:12-16

(q) Zechariah 14:1-4; II Thessalonians 2:8; Revelation 19:11-20

(r) Isaiah 11:1-13; Ezekiel 28:25-26; 34:23-31; Zechariah 14:16; Revelation 20:4-6

(s) Revelation 20:7-9; 21:1-7 and chapter 22

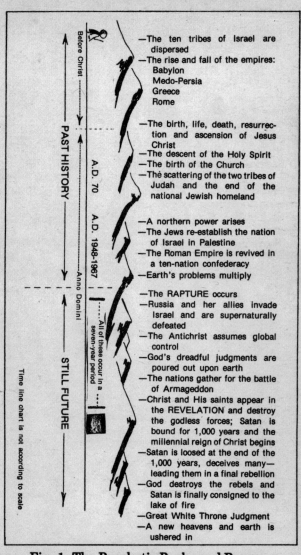

Before Christ

PAST HISTORY

A.D. 70

A.D. 1948-1967

Anno Domini

STILL FUTURE

Time line chart is not according to scale

—The ten tribes of Israel are dispersed
—The rise and fall of the empires:
    Babylon
    Medo-Persia
    Greece
    Rome

—The birth, life, death, resurrection and ascension of Jesus Christ
—The descent of the Holy Spirit
—The birth of the Church
—The scattering of the two tribes of Judah and the end of the national Jewish homeland

—A northern power arises
—The Jews re-establish the nation of Israel in Palestine
—The Roman Empire is revived in a ten-nation confederacy
—Earth's problems multiply

—The RAPTURE occurs
—Russia and her allies invade Israel and are supernaturally defeated
—The Antichrist assumes global control
—God's dreadful judgments are poured out upon earth
—The nations gather for the battle of Armageddon
—Christ and His saints appear in the REVELATION and destroy the godless forces; Satan is bound for 1,000 years and the millennial reign of Christ begins
—Satan is loosed at the end of the 1,000 years, deceives many—leading them in a final rebellion
—God destroys the rebels and Satan is finally consigned to the lake of fire
—Great White Throne Judgment
—A new heavens and earth is ushered in

All of these occur in a seven-year period

Fig. 1: The Prophetic Peaks and Ranges

PART THREE

Final Fulfillment—and its Signs

Coming events cast their shadows before them—and unquestionably the setting sun of earth's ''twenty-ninth day'' causes the long, long shadows of fulfilled prophecy to stretch out behind many of the events occurring right now around our troubled globe.

4

The Pieces Start to Fit Together

It was the week after Christmas.

Brad and Bryan, my two youngest sons, and I were huddled around a table—"hooked" on completing a huge circular picture puzzle, a Christmas gift to one of the boys. We had made excellent progress until, at a particularly difficult spot, we seemed to be stymied by dozens of "look-alike" pieces.

Then Brad spotted it.

Triumphantly he put into place a key piece which, in effect, unlocked a whole series of connections, leading quickly to the completion of the puzzle.

It's a bit like that in terms of prophecy.

To many, the entire complexion of prophecy today is like a gigantic puzzle—with hundreds of pieces that, in a lot of cases, look very much like those which have appeared in the past.

It was like that for Ann, a pert but skeptical young college student with whom I was engaged in conversation about one of my favorite topics—prophecy. In the course of our discussion, I had mentioned a number of the indications of prophetic fulfillment which we'll be considering throughout the rest of this section—factors like the rise of certain nations, Israel's national identity and position in the world, as well as numerous physical and sociological phenomena.

After a period of this sort of conversation, Ann, in a tone that suggested she was surely delivering the ultimate squelch, said, "But after all, most of those things aren't really new. There have always been wars and famines. Earthquakes! And people as far back as the Dark Ages thought that 'signs' in the heavens were a sure forecast of 'the end.' So how can you really believe that these things you're telling me about now are unique enough to seriously suggest that all of these prophecies are going to come to pass?"

That's an intelligent question, and it deserves an honest answer.

It *is* true that throughout human history, there have been lots of times when famine, pestilence, wars, unusual occurrences in the heavens and many similar events have taken place.

70

Moreover, on numerous occasions, certain political alignments have been considered by ill-advised prophetic preachers or writers to be indicators of the culmination of human affairs. I had at one time in my personal library an obscure book, published at the turn of the century, which predicted the British Empire, of all things, to be the vehicle through which the Antichrist would rise to world power.

Others, claiming to be able to read the progress of humanity year by year from an elaborate system based on certain measurements of passages in the Great Pyramid of Egypt, have been contradicted by the passage of time, and their calculations proven in error. Similar embarrassing examples could be multiplied almost endlessly.

But, as I explained to Ann, *there really is a difference now.*

IT'S AN ENTIRELY DIFFERENT BALL GAME

In the first place, though events *similar* to current prophetic signposts have occurred previously, nothing from the past equals the *scale* on which biblical prophetic indicators are appearing today—an aspect about which we'll have more to say later.

But far more important than that is the fact that certain key pieces in the prophetic puzzle have only recently turned up—and it's an entirely different situation today.

71

The key piece, without question, is the nation of Israel. The fact that there even is a modern Israel, with a national homeland, isn't just a twentieth century miracle. It is a most significant prophetic fulfillment in itself, which opens the way to a whole flood of fulfillments.

Jesus said, "When you see the fig tree and all the trees shooting out their leaves, you know that summer is near." (In Scripture, the fig tree has always been a symbol of the nation of Israel.)

Jesus then went on to explain His parable. "So, likewise, when you see these things [things we'll be considering—related to Israel and the nations] come to pass, know that the kingdom of God is near at hand."

He then added that the generation which saw this key event occur would not pass away until all was fulfilled:

> And he spake to them a parable;
> Behold the fig tree, and all the trees;
> When they now shoot forth, ye see
> and know of your own selves that
> summer is now nigh at hand. Verily I
> say unto you, This generation shall
> not pass away, till all be fulfilled.
> Heaven and earth shall pass away:
> but my words shall not pass away
> (Luke 21:29-33).

That's how significant the regathering and nationhood of Israel is—it gives an entirely unique dimension to *all* prophetic events. In chapter five, we'll look in depth at the absolute miracle of Israel's existence. She *really* shouldn't exist—but she does. The only explanation for Israel is that God acted in fulfillment of prophecy.

RUSSIA—AND HER GANG

Then, there's the rise of Russia to world power and the alignment of certain other blocs of nations, *including* the previously improbable Israeli-Egyptian peace treaty. These, too, are key factors which have been clearly spelled out by the prophets. It's virtually impossible to mistake such national entities, because in many instances the nations involved are actually identified by name.

That's why preachers or writers who in the past ignored these key pieces to the puzzle, and who made predictions that did not take these prophecies into account, wound up with egg on their faces.

IT HELPS TO HAVE THE KEY

An understanding of the amazing significance of Israel's nationhood also explains how, decades ago, biblical students like Sir Robert Anderson of Scotland Yard, who understood the nature of key signs (like Israel in particular), could write about events future to them in a lot of detail and still be right on target.

Hal Lindsey, author of the all-time prophetic best-seller *The Late Great Planet Earth*, describes the writings of Increase Mather in 1669, Dr. John Cummings, 1864, and James Grant, 1866—all of whom clearly foresaw and emphatically stated that the nationhood of Israel was a prerequisite to the culmination of prophetic events.

So, while it's true that some of the indicators we'll be considering aren't completely new to human affairs, there's a whole new perspective on them because of the emergence of the nation of Israel, as well as several other key factors which are indeed totally unique to our time.

And—to change our figure of speech—these key factors have become catalysts as in a chemical reaction to set in motion a whole chain reaction of other events.

It really is incredible! To be spectators and, in a sense, participants at a time in human history when so much of prophecy—history written in advance—is being literally fulfilled before our very eyes, is absolutely amazing!

As we get evidence (if we will only recognize it) of this fulfillment on our TV screens, on our radios and in our newspaper headlines, we are forced to admit that it really does look like we're moving into earth's final hours.

That prospect is thrilling, in a bittersweet way—or terribly frightening, depending on your perspective.

You *can* have the thrilling outlook.

All things are mortal but the Jew; all other
forces pass, but he remains. What is the
secret of his immortality?

—Mark Twain

5

Israel—Sitting on the World's Hot Spot

I receive the *Jerusalem Post* each week.

This internationally recognized newspaper—
through its various news reports, opinion
articles and even its unique feature cartoon
"Dry Bones"—provides an interesting perspective on the attitude of the people of Israel to
their position in the world.

The continuing, intense debate among the
Israelis, recorded in the pages of the *Post*, over
Israel's fragile security and the best way to
ensure that security soon gives one the
impression that the Israelis themselves are
under no delusions about their precarious
situation. Indeed, they are almost totally
surrounded by nations officially committed to
their destruction.

Israel has become the world's chronic hot
spot.

It's true that from time to time other global crises take priority. But Israel has been, and remains, the world's number one problem area—an issue about which it seems there can be no neutrality. This is a fact the average individual probably does not understand—but which is true nonetheless.

For example, though little known, the world was pushed literally to the very brink of nuclear war at the time of the fourth Israel-Arab confrontation—the Yom Kippur War of 1973—as Lance Lambert carefully documents in his book *Israel: A Secret Documentary*.

That Israel even exists at all is nothing short of miraculous.

To explain why, let's delve briefly into history, after which we'll show how the miracle of Israel's nationhood and survival is *the* key piece in the unfolding of the prophetic puzzle.

THE MIRACLE OF HER BIRTH

Israel as a nation has an amazing, totally unique history dating back nearly 6,000 years. The Bible describes how at the beginning God chose Abraham and promised to make of him a great nation. God also promised to give the nomadic Abraham's children a land for their home. That land was clearly described.

Later, in Egypt, where Abraham's descendents had gone to escape widespread famine, the family of Israel grew and became a nation. Subsequently, under Moses, they escaped what had become cruel bondage, and finally, led by General Joshua, conquered Canaan which became their home—promised to them by God.

Along the way, they were given the Word of God and the divine moral code—in the Ten Commandments and the Pentateuch. God also made it very clear to them, through Moses, that if they obeyed His word His blessing would be theirs, but if they disobeyed, the judgments of the Almighty would be visited upon them. This agreement between God and His people is recorded in the Old Testament book Deuteronomy.

HERE'S THAT AMAZING DOCUMENT

And it shall come to pass, if thou shalt hearken diligently unto the voice of the Lord thy God, to observe and to do all his commandments which I command thee this day, that the Lord thy God will set thee on high above all nations of the earth:

And all these blessings shall come on thee, and overtake thee, if thou shalt hearken unto the voice of the Lord thy God.

Blessed shalt thou be in the city, and blessed shalt thou be in the field.

Blessed shall be the fruit of thy body, and the fruit of thy ground, and the fruit of thy cattle, the increase of thy kine, and the flocks of thy sheep.

Blessed shall be thy basket and thy store.

Blessed shalt thou be when thou comest in, and blessed shalt thou be when thou goest out.

The Lord shall cause thine enemies that rise up against thee to be smitten before thy face: they shall come out against thee one way, and flee before thee seven ways.

The Lord shall command the blessing upon thee in thy storehouses, and in all that thou settest thine hand unto; and he shall bless thee in the land which the Lord thy God giveth thee.

The Lord shall establish thee an holy people unto himself, as he hath sworn unto thee, if thou shalt keep the commandments of the Lord thy God, and walk in his ways,

And all people of the earth shall see that thou art called by the name of the Lord; and they shall be afraid of thee.

And the Lord shall make thee plenteous in goods, in the fruit of thy body, and in the fruit of thy cattle, and in the fruit of thy ground, in the land which the Lord sware unto thy fathers to give thee.

The Lord shall open unto thee his good treasure, the heaven to give the rain unto the land in his season, and to bless all the work of thine hand: and thou shalt lend unto many nations, and thou shalt not borrow.

And the Lord shall make thee the head, and not the tail; and thou shalt be above only, and thou shalt not be beneath; if that thou hearken unto the commandments of the Lord thy God, which I command thee this day, to observe and to do them:

And thou shalt not go aside from any of the words which I command thee this day, to the right hand, or to the left, to go after other gods to serve them.

But it shall come to pass, if thou wilt not hearken unto the voice of the Lord thy God, to observe to do all his commandments and his statutes which I command thee this day; that all these curses shall come upon thee, and overtake thee:

Cursed shalt thou be in the city, and cursed shalt thou be in the field.

Cursed shall be thy basket and thy store.

Cursed shall be the fruit of body, and the fruit of thy land, the increase of thy kine, and the flocks of thy sheep.

Cursed shalt thou be when thou comest in, and cursed shalt thou be when thou goest out.

The Lord shall send upon thee cursing, vexation, and rebuke, in all that thou settest thine hand unto for to do, until thou be destroyed, and until thou perish quickly; because of the wickedness of thy doings, whereby thou hast forsaken me.

The Lord shall make the pestilence cleave unto thee, until he have consumed thee from off the land, whither thou goest to possess it.

The Lord shall smite thee with a consumption, and with a fever, and with an inflammation, and with an extreme burning, and with the sword, and with blasting, and with mildew; and they shall pursue thee until thou perish....

Thy sons and thy daughters shall be given unto another people, and thine eyes shall look, and fail with longing for them all the day long: and there shall be no might in thine hand.

The fruit of thy land, and all thy labors, shall a nation which thou knowest not eat up; and thou shalt be only oppressed and crushed alway:

So that thou shalt be mad for the sight of thine eyes which thou shalt see.

The Lord shall smite thee in the

knees, and in the legs, with a sore both that cannot be healed, from the sole of thy foot unto the top of thy head.

The Lord shall bring thee, and thy king which thou shalt set over thee, unto a nation which neither thou nor thy fathers have known; and there shalt thou serve other gods, wood and stone.

And thou shalt become an astonishment, a proverb, and a byword, among all nations whither the Lord shall lead thee....

The stranger that is within thee shall get up above thee very high; and thou shalt come down very low.

He shall lend to thee, and thou shalt not lend to him: he shall be the head; and thou shalt be the tail.

Moreover all these curses shall come upon thee, and shall pursue thee, and overtake thee, till thou be destroyed; because thou hearkenedst not unto the voice of the Lord thy God, to keep his commandments and his statutes which he commanded thee:

And they shall be upon thee for a sign and for a wonder, and upon thy seed for ever.

Because thou servedst not the Lord thy God with joyfulness, and with gladness of heart, for the abundance of all things....

The Lord shall bring a nation against thee from far, from the end of the earth, as swift as the eagle flieth; a nation whose tongue thou shalt not understand;

A nation of fierce countenance, which shall not regard the person of the old, nor shew favor to the young:

And he shall eat the fruit of thy cattle, and the fruit of thy land, until thou be destroyed: which also shall not leave thee either corn, wine, or oil, or the increase of thy kine, or flocks of thy sheep, until he have destroyed thee.

And he shall besiege thee in all thy gates, until thy high and fenced walls come down, wherein thou trustedst, throughout all thy land: and he shall besiege thee in all thy gates throughout all thy land, which the Lord thy God hath given thee.

And thou shalt eat the fruit of thine own body, the flesh of thy sons and of thy daughters, which the Lord thy God hath given thee, in the siege, and in the straitness, wherewith thine enemies shall distress thee....

If thou wilt not observe to do all the words of this law that are written in this book, that thou mayest fear this glorious and fearful name, THE LORD THY GOD;

Then the Lord will make thy plagues wonderful, and the plagues of thy seed, even great plagues, and of long continuance, and sore sicknesses, and of long continuance.

Moreover he will bring upon thee all the diseases of Egypt, which thou wast afraid of; and they shall cleave unto thee.

Also every sickness, and every plague, which is not written in the book of this law, them will the Lord bring upon thee, until thou be destroyed.

And ye shall be left few in number, whereas ye were as the stars of heaven for multitude; because thou wouldest not obey the voice of the Lord thy God.

And it shall come to pass, that as the Lord rejoiced over you to do you good, and to multiply you; so the Lord will rejoice over you to destroy you, and to bring you to nought; and ye shall be plucked from off the land whither thou goest to possess it.

And the Lord shall scatter thee among all people, from the one end of the earth even unto the other; and there thou shalt serve other gods, which neither thou nor thy fathers have known, even wood and stone.

And among these nations shalt thou find no ease, neither shall the sole of thy foot have rest: but the Lord shall give thee there a trembling heart, and failing of eyes, and sorrow of mind:

And thy life shall hang in doubt before thee; and thou shalt fear day and night, and shalt have none assurance of thy life:

In the morning thou shalt say, Would God it were even! and at even thou shalt say, Would God it were morning! for the fear of thine heart wherewith thou shalt fear, and for the sight of thine eyes which thou shalt see.

And the Lord shall bring thee into Egypt again with ships, by the way whereof I spake unto thee, Thou shalt see it no more again: and there ye shall be sold unto your enemies for bondmen and bondwomen, and no man shall buy you.

These are the words of the covenant, which the Lord commanded Moses to make with the children of Israel in the land of Moab, beside the covenant which he made with them in Horeb.

Deuteronomy 28:1-22, 32-37, 43-47, 49-53, 58-68, 29:1

THE TRAGIC CYCLE

History records the tragic story. National

disobedience to God's laws, followed by His judgment, followed by repentance and God's promised aid, followed by disobedience, became a continuous cycle. The nation went steadily downhill spiritually—*and* in every other way!

Finally, the chosen people were divided into two nations—the ten tribes of Israel to the north, and the two tribes of Judah in the south.

These two nations lived side by side for 200 years, often engaging in war between themselves, as well as with the nations around them.

Meanwhile, their national disregard for God, worse in Israel, continued and became so great that finally divine judgment permitted Israel's complete destruction as a nation—with her people carried away into a captivity from which they would not return for centuries.

Judah, the southern nation, also experienced the judgment of God for her sin and was later conquered by a succession of enemies, though permitted to remain in the land.

Later, under the Macabees, a Jewish state did exist for a brief time about 140 B.C. until the armies of Rome conquered all of the then-known world, including Judah.

During His earthly ministry, Jesus Christ, who lived and was crucified under Roman dominion, added to the prophetic forecast on Israel. He said:

87

And when ye shall see Jerusalem
compassed with armies, then know that
the desolation thereof is nigh.

Then let them which are in Judea flee
to the mountains; and let them which
are in the midst of it depart out; and let
not them that are in the countries enter
thereinto.

For these be the days of vengeance,
that all things which are written may be
fulfilled.

And they shall fall by the edge of the
sword, and shall be led away captive
into all nations: and Jerusalem shall be
trodden down of the Gentiles, until the
times of the Gentiles be fulfilled.

Luke 21:20-24

That prophecy was literally fulfilled when in
A.D. 70—as a "final solution to the Jewish
problem"—the Roman general Titus brutally
put down a rebellion, crucified hundreds upon
thousands of Jews, sold thousands more into
slavery in other lands and totally destroyed
Jerusalem, even razing the Temple by fire. [17]

A band of about 1,000 Jewish soldiers,
women and children did hold out against the
might of Rome for months in the desert
stronghold of Masada, but when that heroic
community finally fell in A.D. 100, the nation of
Israel literally ceased to exist. [18]

Her people were dispersed among the

nations. Her national homeland, in ruins and desolate, was under the control of others. Just as God said. You can read it in the history books.

THE MIRACLE OF HER PRESERVATION

Now it's a fact that when a people are deprived of a homeland and dispersed among various nations for any length of time, they usually soon lose their national identity. It happens even when the dispersal is voluntary. The melting pot that is America is a graphic illustration of this. People from England, Ireland, France, Germany, Holland, Poland, Mexico—the world—have come to America, and in less than 200 years there has been such a blending of nationalities and races that a "new" people has emerged.

In many of the South American and Southeast Asian countries, this kind of blending has, in just 3-400 years, made it difficult to detect original ancestries.

But consider the Jews!

Deprived of self-government for some 2,500 years, and without a national homeland for nearly twenty centuries, still they have maintained their distinctive nationality.

The magnitude of this phenomenon is increased when the Jews are compared to other contemporary nationalities. Where are the

Assyrians, the Babylonians, the Hittites or Amalekites today? They were great nations at one time, often controlling the then-known world. In fact, at the time that the Jews were conquered by the Babylonians, it is estimated that the Jews numbered less than 100,000— while their captors, who ruled their world, were many times that population.

Yet today the Jew lives on—the Babylonians are gone.

Mark Twain, certainly not a religious man, observed and commented on this amazing phenomenon in a quotation which appears in *The World's Greatest Library*. He wrote:

> He [the Jew] could be...vain of himself and not be ashamed of it. Yes, he could be excused for it. The Egyptian, the Babylonian, and the Persian arose, filled the planet with sound and splendor, then faded to dream-stuff, and passed away; the Greek and the Roman followed, and made a fast noise, and they are gone; other peoples have sprung up and held the torch high for a time; but it burned out, and they sit in twilight, or have vanished. The Jew saw them all, and is now what he always was, exhibiting no decadence, no infirmities of age, no weakening of his parts, no slowing of his energies, no dulling of his alert, aggressive mind. All

things are mortal but the Jew; all other forces pass, but he remains. What is the secret of his immortality? [19]

The secret is that God *has spoken* concerning the Jew, and He is keeping His Word...supernaturally.

THE MIRACLE OF HER NATIONHOOD

But the Jew has not merely retained his national identity, miraculous as that is. He has regained and is actually in his original homeland—against unbelievable odds.

After the Jews were dispersed, a succession of nations controlled Palestine. The Romans ruled until A.D. 611, when the Persians swept over the land. They in turn gave way to the Islamic armies of Saladin in 637, during whose rule the Muslim Dome of the Rock was constructed in Jerusalem.

The Crusaders captured Jerusalem in 1099 and held it till 1187, when the Moslems of the area recaptured it. The Ottoman Turks overpowered them in 1291 and held the land until December of 1917, when General Allenby and his British forces captured Jerusalem without firing a shot. World War I thus opened Palestine for the return of the Jews.

Meanwhile, in the late nineteenth century, the Jewish Nationalist movement known as

Zionism was born in Eastern Europe. The Jews who had often suffered violence in various places through the centuries, lived in fear of the periodic Russian pogroms. When brutal massacres actually were unleashed, the drive for a return to Palestine was accelerated.

And it had to be *Palestine*. In 1903, the British Government offered the Zionists territory in Uganda, then a British possession, but they turned it down, emphatically insisting that they must return to the promised land of their forefathers—Palestine.

Some began to go back. By the end of the 1800s there were approximately 5,000 Jews in Palestine, pioneers who settled in marshlands and barren areas, purchased from absentee Arab owners. The earliest Jewish towns and villages were built by them from 1880 to 1922. In 1909, Deganiah ("The Cornflower") was founded by ten men and two women as the first "kibbutz"—a Jewish collective settlement. It became the forerunner of nearly 400 such present day collectives. Begun on a swampy fringe of the Jordan River, Deganiah today stands as a showpiece of modern Israel—surrounded by orchards, gardens and green fields of corn and vegetables.

By 1914, the Jewish population had risen to 85,000. In 1916, during the time when Palestine was the theater of furious fighting during World War I, the British were given control of Palestine and Iran under an agreement with

France.

When General Allenby actually captured Jerusalem in 1917, the Balfour Declaration was put into effect. In this historic document, Britain said she would "view with favor the establishment *in Palestine* of a *national home for the Jewish people* and would use her best efforts to facilitate the achievement of this objective."

However, when Jews began to return in slow but steadily-increasing numbers, tensions between them and the Palestinian Arabs frequently erupted into overt conflict. In 1939, Britain, in the middle of the conflict and frustrated by it, issued a White Paper that favored Arab independence and control. In 1946, immigration of more Jews was forbidden, and finally in 1947, the British withdrew from Palestine.

Hostilities flared between the Jews and Arabs. The United Nations stepped in, partitioned the country and sought to keep the peace. Shortly thereafter, the Jewish National Council and the General Zionist Council proclaimed from Tel Aviv the establishment of the Sovereign State of Israel. David Ben Gurion was appointed prime minister and Dr. Chaim Weizmann was elected president of a provisional council.

Both the United States and Russia recognized the new nation which, after much debate, was accepted as a member nation into the United

Nations. And so, on May 14, 1949, Israel became again a nation with her own homeland and national flag. [20]

THE MIRACLE OF HER SURVIVAL

But the miracle did not end with Israel's achievement of nationhood. The young nation's survival through *four* devastating wars is certainly as great a miracle, if not a greater one.

Immediately after Israel's declaration of independence and statehood, the small, weak, recently-formed nation of less that three-quarters of a million people was plunged into a life-and-death struggle for its very survival. The neighboring Arab states were not, and in most cases have not since been, willing to acknowledge Israel as a sovereign power with a right to Palestine. They attacked Israel.

It should have been no contest. In the natural, Israel didn't have a hope. The odds against her were overwhelming—and still are.* The

---

* The odds have always been against Israel militarily. A 1974 USAF intelligence report says that over the past fifteen years Arab manpower outweighed Israel's by ten to one, armor by at least five to one, assault weaponry and artillery by five to one or higher, combat aircraft by three to one, munitions stocks and military production ratios by 100 to one. [21]

massive documentary *O Jerusalem* by Larry Collins and Dominique LaPierre graphically tells the story.

But when the "war of independence" ended on January 7, 1949, Israel had not only survived, she had increased substantially her possession of key areas of the country. The U.N. came in to patrol a "no man's land" buffer zone between the Israelis and the Arabs.[22]

However, military and political pressures between the combatants constantly intensified until October 29, 1956, when Israel invaded the Sinai shortly after Egypt nationalized the Suez Canal and denied Israel's ships passage through it.

The invasion, which was supported by Britain and France, was a complete success from the Jewish point of view. In just seven days, before the U.N. established the first international police force to supervise a truce, Israel routed 40,000 Egyptian troops, overran the Sinai and closed the Canal.

Once again a shaky peace ensued, but the cycle of build-up in tension continued. The inevitable eruption came in June 1967 in the famous Six-Day War. That phenomenal Israeli blitz—again against overwhelming odds in terms of manpower and military equipment—saw the Jewish occupation of the entire Sinai, the Golan Heights in Syria, the territory to the Jordan River and, MOST SIGNIFICANTLY—the Old City of Jerusalem.

Thus, in 1967, for the first time in over 1,900 years, the Holy City, with its Temple site, was in Jewish hands. Shortly after the capture of Old Jerusalem, and while the war was still on, General Moshe Dayan marched to the Wailing Wall—that last remnant of the Old Temple—and said, "We have returned to our holiest of Holy places, never to leave again." The prophetic significance of this is enormous, as will be shown later in chapter eight. [23]

Miraculous!

But perhaps the greatest evidence of the miraculous survival of Israel came in the 1973 Yom Kippur War. That war should have seen the annihilation of the state of Israel. Even the late prime minister, Golda Meir, said of that conflict, "For the first time in our 25-year history, we thought we might have lost." [24] At one point, only a few battered Israeli tanks stood between the powerful Egyptian army and Tel Aviv. At the same time, the Syrian massed tanks had all of Galilee at their mercy, with virtually nothing to stop them from advance.

The Israelis perhaps had become over-confident following their previous confrontations with the Arabs. A prevailing Jewish attitude was, "All you have to do is fire a few shots in the air and the Syrians run like rabbits. Just point a tank in the direction of Cairo, and the Egyptians collapse immediately." [25]

So Israel was taken by surprise. The attack came on the Jewish high holy day. Many in the nation of Israel were observing the day in the synagogues or in prayer and fasting. With the Arabs united for the first time in centuries, powerfully equipped with the lastest sophisticated weapons and attacking on two fronts simultaneously, it appeared that Israel was indeed beaten.

The Arab assault was massive. In the north, the Syrians threw 1,200 tanks into a twenty-mile front, 25 percent more tanks than the Germans used in a 200-mile offensive against Russia in 1941! [26] What has been called "the greatest tank battle in world history" was fought in the Sinai. According to news reports at the time, approximately 4,000 tanks, over 2,000 heavy guns, hundreds of missile batteries, 1,500 aircraft and nearly one million men as well as many unproven new weapons were thrown at Israel at the start of the war. It was the Middle East's first truly technological war. [27]

Not only were the Israelis vastly outnumbered, but the Arab weapons were also superior—with the very latest, including surface to air (SAM) missiles, and other newly developed weaponry having been supplied to them by Russia. In addition, massive Soviet airlifts of arms to Syria and Egypt began on the first day of the war. Two hours after the fighting started, Russian Antonov transports, carrying weapons and replacements, began landing every three minutes at Syria's airport. Russian supply ships came into port in both countries.

On the other hand, the American airlift to Israel did not begin until the tenth day of the war, due to the refusal of America's allies to grant facilities to the U.S. for the refueling of planes. When the U.S. planes finally did arrive, the Israeli army was actually running out of ammunition.[28] Israel's casualties in the first few days of the war were enormous. A comparable loss in the U.S. would have been 200,000 lives; in Canada, 20,000.

To fully tell the entire story of Israel's "miracle" survival and victory of sorts, including the account of how the U.S. and Russia went to the very brink of nuclear war over the conflict, would take an entire book.

In fact, several have been written. Lance Lambert, a British citizen who was in Israel during the war and who spends a great deal of time there, vividly but in a sane, balanced way, describes that miracle in his excellent book *Israel: A Secret Documentary*.

There is no logical explanation for the failure of Egypt and Syria to totally destroy Israel during the Yom Kippur War or for Jordan to refuse to attack—a factor which undoubtedly would have been decisive.

The fact is that after the Egyptians had taken the supposedly invincible Bar-Lev line in a third of the time they had projected for its capture, and after the Syrian tanks had a clear run from the Golan Heights into Israel—*they both inexplicably just stopped.* [29]

Many feel that those unexplainable delays gave Israel the time it *had* to have to recover from the surprise, regroup and reorganize. This factor almost certainly made the difference in the outcome of the war.

Whether this is true or not, the fact remains that Israel's very survival through the Yom Kippur War is a miracle. Many Israelis themselves agree: it had to be God.

Since then, terrorism in Israel continues (a volunteer Civil Guard of over 100,000 exists in Israel, set up to combat increased PLO terror attacks after 1973), Russia threatens and, in spite of the Egyptian peace treaty, the Arab world presses for Israel's annihilation.

THE MIRACLE OF HER PRODUCTIVITY

A less dramatic but nonetheless real miracle is the fulfillment of prophecy concerning Israel's productivity, after *centuries* of desolation. The prophetic word to Israel foretold desolation upon the land because of their disobedience.

> And if ye will not for all this hearken unto me, but walk contrary unto me...I will bring the land into desolation: and your enemies which dwell therein shall be astonished at it.
> And I will scatter you among the

heathen, and will draw out a sword after you: and your land shall be desolate, and your cities waste.

Leviticus 26: 27, 32, 33

Therefore, ye mountains of Israel, hear the word of the Lord God; Thus saith the Lord God to the mountains, and to the hills, to the rivers, and to the valleys, to the desolate wastes, and to the cities that are forsaken, which became a prey and derision to the residue of the heathen that are round about.

Ezekiel 36: 4

For hundreds of years this was so. Mark Twain's verdict on Palestine after his visit there in the 1870s was, "Forbidding desolation." Erosion, deteriorating terrains, malarial swamps, with little vegetation to be found anywhere—this was the description he gave.

Very few inhabitants were in the land—until after the turn of the century. Exactly as prophesied. But restoration was also foretold.

But ye, O mountains of Israel, ye shall shoot forth your branches, and yield your fruit to my people of Israel; for they are at hand to come.

For, behold, I am for you, and I will turn unto you, and ye shall be tilled and sown:

And I will multiply upon you man and beast; and they shall increase and bring fruit: and I will settle you after your old estates, and will do better unto you than at your beginnings: and ye shall know that I am the Lord.

Ezekiel 36:8,9 and 11

I will also save you from all your uncleannesses: and I will call for the corn, and will increase it, and lay no famine upon you.

And I will multiply the fruit of the tree, and the increase of the field, that ye shall receive no more reproach of famine among the heathen.

And the desolate land shall be tilled, whereas it lay desolate in the sight of all that passed by.

And they shall say, This land that was desolate is become like the garden of Eden; and the waste and desolate and ruined cities are become fenced, and are inhabited.

Ezekiel 36:29,30,34,35

Today these prophecies are literally coming true. Since Israel has achieved statehood, millions of trees have been planted, covering hundreds of thousands of acres. Swamps have been drained, sand dunes anchored with vegetation, erosion combatted, soil improved and massive irrigation undertaken.

Agriculture has been modernized and crops of corn, wheat, cotton, peanuts, sugar beets and nuts are harvested. The nation produces more than 70 percent of its own food supply.

Israel has become the world's second largest producer of grapefruit. Her oranges are world famous. Grapes, bananas, dates, lemons and other fruit are grown and exported, as well as enormous quantities of vegetables. Isaiah 27:6's pronouncement, "Israel shall blossom and bud and fill the face of the world with fruit," appears to be seeing fulfillment.

Other products include olives, almonds, figs, apricots and pomegranates. Flowers and flower bulbs are also grown and exported—literally hundreds of millions each year. [30]

In addition, Israel—which now has a population approaching 3.5 million, about one-third of whom are native born "sabras" —also has very progressive mineral and manufacturing industries and produces about ten percent of her oil needs. She is also very actively into solar energy research and development.

A great deal more could be said about the miracle that is Israel today. Documentation could fill a book.

The point of all of this is that, in a very special way, a regathered, prosperous nation of Israel is *the* most significant sign of prophecy's impending fulfillment. In chapter four we referred to the parable Jesus told about the fig tree—the historic symbol of national Israel— putting forth its leaves, indicating that summer was near. Jesus told that parable as part of his answer to the disciples' questions, "What will be the sign of your coming?" and "What will be the sign of the end of the age?" (Matthew 24).

In the first part of His answer to those questions, Jesus described many general world conditions, like wars, famines and earthquakes, which He said would increase in frequency and intensity like labor pangs prior to the birth of a child. We'll look at some of these signs in chapter ten.

Then, as a *major* part of His response, Jesus spoke of Israel being back in the land of Palestine (Matthew 24:16) with the Temple rebuilt (Matthew 24:15) and with even their ancient worship restored (Matthew 24:20)— following, of course, a lengthy worldwide dispersion.

Then Jesus foretold that the generation which saw Israel reborn (the "fig tree putting forth its leaves"*) would not pass away until all these

------

* The nation of Israel has taken as its national tree the fig tree.

things came to pass (Matthew 24:34).

So the miracle of Israel's rebirth has occurred. And, in spite of all the odds against it, Israel still exists, and *will continue to do so*—supernaturally. Read Jeremiah 31:35-36 for the *guarantee from God!*

Just as the appearance of leaves on the trees is a sure sign that summer is near, so the emergence of Israel and its position right on the world's hot spot is certain proof that Jesus Christ will soon return and the culmination of earth's history will be upon us.

The budding of the fig tree (a Jewish nation reborn in Palestine, controlling for the first time in more than two millenia the city of the Temple) is the key piece of the prophetic jigsaw puzzle slipping into place and making possible the placing of the many adjacent pieces.

It's an exciting time to be alive.

For Further Reading:

Israel: A Secret Documentary by Lance Lambert

Encyclopedia Britannica—Vols. 12,13,17 [1958 Edition]

Events among the nations of earth—the
Arab oil producers, the European Common
Market, China, and Russia—appear to be
rapidly taking shape in the pattern that was
foretold. The "pieces of the puzzle"
adjacent to Israel seem to be falling into
place.

6

The Nations Are Astir

Ten years ago no one would have believed it.

In the late 60s and even early 70s, most
people thought of the Arab nations as rather
backward desert countries ruled by fabulously
wealthy sheiks—right out of *The Arabian
Nights*. Today those Arabs—the majority of the
OPEC nations—comprise one of the most
powerful groups of nations in the world.

Oil has done it.

One of the important results of the 1973
Arab-Israeli war was to bring the Arab world
into a new and unprecedented unity—one based
primarily on its control of most of the oil
resources of the world.

That unity is obviously related to their major
goal: the destruction of Israel. From the
standpoint of the Arab nations, the presence of
Israel in the Middle East is a cancerous sore

which can be cured only by radical surgery. That is why the dramatic Egyptian-Israeli peace treaty, which we'll consider in chapter seven, caused such an Arab outcry against Egypt for daring to betray the Arab cause.

THE PALESTINIAN PROBLEM

It may also explain why the hundreds of thousands of Palestinian refugees—those people and their descendants who were allegedly forced out of Palestine when Israel became a nation—are kept in such squalor. Many observers believe that they are merely a political football, since with the vast OPEC wealth and their great tracts of unused land, the Arab nations could easily resettle the Palestinians.

Moshe Sharon, in an August 24, 1979, *Jerusalem Post* article, writes convincingly about the economic and political "necessity" which the Palestinian problem has become to the Arab States. [31] However, just as Israel clung to its hope of the Promised Land, so the Arab world has clung to its hope of driving Israel into the Mediterranean Sea and restoring the entire land, including Jerusalem, to Arab control.

Little wonder that the Israelis have a sense of concern over their national security! To the Arabs it seems only a matter of time until their vastly superior numbers and rapidly increasing wealth make the final defeat of Israel a certainty.

And oil is a major Arab weapon.

The whole world has felt the effect of the OPEC nations' use of this weapon. Since November 1973, when the Arab oil-producing nations (who in 1972 owned two-thirds of the world's proved oil reserves) reduced their production and attempted to embargo nations which favored Israel, there has been an entirely new global situation. [32]

A NEW WAR IS ON

A new war is in progress—an economic war with far-reaching implications for the world and for Israel. The gloomy prospect of insufficient fuel for homes, industry, and the military has sent shock waves around the globe. The regular price increases since 1973 have made every consumer throughout the industrialized nations aware, at least in his pocket book, of the grim facts of this new era. Runaway inflation, fueled (pardon the pun) by these actions, is a related and very serious problem. For the first time in centuries, the Arab nations of the Middle East have become a *major* component in *every* international consideration.

While the oil and energy crisis unquestionably affects all the world, particularly the industrialized nations, the area most seriously hit is Europe. Europe, along with Japan and the smaller emerging nations, is far more vulnerable to manipulation than either the U.S. or Russia. The U.S. is considered to have the potential of a high degree of self-sufficiency in oil, though admittedly at a tremendous cost. The whole oil issue, however, could spell a real decline in power and influence for the U.S.—an effect which many believe is already occurring.

What prophetic significance does all of this have?

First, a revived Roman Empire has been prophesied, including a good part of Europe down to the Mediterranean. The rise of the OPEC countries to power and their use of oil as a weapon are further serving to forge this ten-nation European entity, which figures so predominantly in end-time events, as the next section of this chapter describes.

Second, the prophets foresaw, at the time of the end, a "king of the south" who appears in end-time battles (Daniel 11). Many scholars believe this to be a reference to an Arab confederacy. The Arab emergence as a dominant world force fits this.

Third, another projected effect of the oil situation appears to be a further push by Russia in the direction of cultivating the Arab nations and uniting with them against Israel (as prophesied—and the subject of chapter seven).

Fourth, if in fact the global oil situation does contribute to America's continued and more rapid decline as a world power, this also fits into the prophetic picture, since the U.S. plays very little, if any, role in prophecies concerning the last days.

Let's look in more detail now at that ten-nation confederacy.

THE ROMAN EMPIRE—REVIVED

In 1957, in the city of Rome, a treaty was signed which I believe was the beginning of the fulfillment of a major prophecy by the renowned prophet Daniel, given in Babylon back in about 600 B.C. Let's look at the prophecy first and then the reasons why many scholars believe we are seeing its fulfillment now.

A dream precipitated it all. King Nebuchadnezzar, ruler of Babylon the Great, had a dream one night and demanded that his wise men, astrologers, and sorcerers interpret it for him. The only problem was that he couldn't recall the dream. Nevertheless, he insisted that his counsellors, in spite of their protests, reveal *both* the dream *and* its meaning—or be put to death!

At the last moment, Daniel, the godly young Hebrew captive, was called in. Through a revelation from God in answer to prayer, Daniel was able to describe the dream and interpret its meaning.

The dream was about a great statue,

overwhelming in its size. It had a head of gold, chest and arms of silver, abdomen and thighs of brass, and legs of iron, with feet part clay and part iron.

Then, in the dream, a stone (which was cut supernaturally without hands out of a mountain) came and struck the statue on its feet. The image was crushed and demolished so that no trace of it remained, while the stone began to increase in size until it filled all the earth.

Daniel's interpretation followed. In summary, Daniel declared that God had given dominion to Gentile powers—four of which were to rise and govern the world. But in the latter time of the fourth power, the God of heaven would establish a kingdom which would supercede all other earthly kingdoms and endure forever. Here is the biblical record:

> This is the dream; and we will tell the interpretation thereof before the king.
> Thou, O king, art a king of kings: for the God of heaven hath given thee a kingdom, power, and strength, and glory.
> And wheresoever the children of men dwell, the beasts of the field and the fowls of the heaven hath he given into thine hand, and hath made thee ruler over them all. Thou art this head of gold.
> And after thee shall arise another

kingdom inferior to thee, and another third kingdom of brass, which shall bear rule over all the earth.

And the fourth kingdom shall be strong as iron: forasmuch as iron breaketh in pieces and subdueth all things: and as iron that breaketh all these, shall it break in pieces and bruise.

And whereas thou sawest the feet and toes, part of potters' clay, and part of iron, the kingdom shall be divided; but there shall be in it of the strength of the iron, forasmuch as thou sawest the iron mixed with miry clay.

And as the toes of the feet were part of iron, and part of clay, so the kingdom shall be partly strong, and partly broken.

And whereas thou sawest iron mixed with miry clay, they shall mingle themselves with the seed of men: but they shall not cleave one to another, even as iron is not mixed with clay.

And in the days of these kings shall the God of heaven set up a kingdom, which shall never be destroyed: and the kingdom shall not be left to other people, but it shall break in pieces and consume all these kingdoms, and it shall stand for ever.

Forasmuch as thou sawest that the

stone was cut out of the mountain without hands, and that it brake in pieces the iron, the brass, the clay, the silver, and the gold; the great God hath made known to the king what shall come to pass hereafter: and the dream is certain, and the interpretation thereof sure.   Daniel 2:36-45

Daniel's word to Nebuchadnezzar was "*You are this head of gold*" (2:38). The golden head, then, symbolized the Babylonian empire... appropriately enough, since the capital was called "the golden city" and the empire was indeed grand and great.

"After you will arise another kingdom inferior to you" (2:39), Daniel continued, represented by the silver chest and arms. In 539 B.C. the Medo-Persian armies conquered Babylon and became supreme. Though a larger kingdom geographically, it was in many ways inferior to Babylon, even as silver is inferior to gold. And it did have *two* parts, symbolized by the *two arms*.

"And another third kingdom of brass which shall bear rule over all the earth" (2:39). The empire of Greece under Alexander the Great, who decreed that he be called "King of all the world," defeated Persia in 331 B.C. His kingdom extended from India to Egypt and Europe. That empire was symbolized by the abdomen and thighs, as Daniel 8:20,21 makes clear.

"And the fourth kingdom shall be strong as iron" (2:40). The two iron legs of the statue represented the power which succeeded Greece—Rome. In 63 B.C. the Romans conquered all the lands surrounding the Mediterranean and ruled until A.D. 476. They imposed the *Pax Romana*—the Roman peace—a peace enforced by the iron heel of Rome, stamping out all freedom in the process. The Roman rule was marked by great strength which crushed and demolished resistance. It also corresponded to the two legs—through its division into eastern and western branches.

This much is history, or prophecy already fulfilled. It is possible to look back upon these empires and to observe the ruins of their rules. [33]

But what about the feet and toes of the statue—the final form of the Roman Empire? And what about the stone that pulverized the image and then filled the earth?

It must be understood that the scope of Daniel's prophecy extends from the time of Nebuchadnezzar to the time of Christ's return to set up *His* kingdom upon earth. Quite obviously, there is a major time gap between verses 40 and 41. Daniel 2:37-40 is ancient history which we can clearly identify. Verses 41-45 are obviously yet to be fulfilled. When will this occur?

This prophetic dream was clearly indicating that the Roman Empire would go into eclipse after a dramatic history, to reappear at the time immediately preceding the return of Jesus Christ. The concept of a resurrected Rome is not a new one. Mussolini, for one, believed in it and sought vainly to effect its revival. Napoleon before him obviously entertained grandiose ideas of a new empire. So did Hitler, who borrowed the term Reich, calling it the Third. So how and when will this revived Roman Empire come into being?

Several additional clues are available to us from a parallel prophetic passage in Daniel. Chapter 7 covers the same prophetic period, but from a different perspective. It has been well-observed that Nebuchadnezzar's dream saw human events from *man's* perspective—a grand statue. Daniel 7, which describes four beasts arising from the sea, is said to be *God's* view of human government—seen as He does in its violent, rapacious, beastly nature.

The message in Daniel 7 confirms and adds detail to what the dream in chapter 2 revealed. Especially is this true of the revised form of the Roman Empire. Note the prophecy:

> Thus he said, the fourth beast shall be the fourth kingdom upon the earth,

which shall be diverse from all kingdoms, and shall devour the whole earth, and shall tread it down, and break it in pieces.

And the ten horns out of this kingdom are ten kings that shall arise: and another shall rise after them; and he shall be diverse from the first, and he shall subdue three kings.

And he shall speak great words against the most High, and shall wear out the saints of the most High, and think to change times and laws: and they shall be given into his hand until a time and times and the dividing of time.

Daniel 7:23-25

This new kingdom will be a confederacy of ten kings (7:24) arising out of the first Roman Empire, even as feet and toes come out from legs. It will combine strong and weak nations (7:24) as of iron and clay, and will have severe internal problems until one of the rulers, described elsewhere as the Antichrist, subdues three others and assumes control with a strong hand (7:24,25). It will be in existence at the time when Jesus returns to establish His kingdom (2:45) and will be destroyed by Him (7:26; 2:45; Rev. 19:11-21).

Now, is there anything currently that fits this description—any grouping of ten nations in the geographic area once controlled by Rome?

Of course.

That 1957 Treaty of Rome—begun as an economic partnership—has become, by 1980, the ten-member European Economic Community, better known as the European Common Market. Dr. Walter Hallstein, the former president of the EEC, detailed the vision of a United Europe some years ago when he wrote:

> Three phases of the European unification are to be noted. First, the customs union, second, the economic union, third, the political union...what we have created on the way to uniting Europe is a mighty economic-political union of which nothing may be sacrificed for any reason. Its value exists not only in what it is, but more in what it promises to become....At about 1980 we may fully expect the great fusion of all economic, military, and political communities together into the United States of Europe.[34]

Hallstein was inaccurate on the *time*, but the

events he forecast are apparently coming to pass.

Elections to a European parliament were held in June 1979 with 410 representatives of nine nations selected. (Greece, the tenth nation, was admitted later in 1979 with full membership to be accorded January 1, 1981.) The first session of the Euro-parliament was held in August 1979 and Simone Veil of France was elected President. The first sessions were stormy and largely non-productive, but in spite of all that, the United States of Europe is definitely off the ground. [35]

A common currency—the "ecu"—was put into use in 1980.

This is a major power block. The Gross National Product of the combined ECM nations is second only to the U.S. Its population is almost equal to that of the U.S. and Russia combined. When and if it resolves internal problems and begins to truly function as a unit, it will be formidable.

It is interesting to superimpose a map of the ten ECM nations over a map of the old Roman Empire. The similarity is striking. Now, this may not be the final form of the revived Roman Empire. Changes could occur—but this alignment definitely must be the forerunner, at the very least, of the complete fulfillment of Daniel's prophecy.

That means Christ's return could be very near.

Another of the nations astir these days is the world's largest—China. With a population of some one billion, the oriental giant is no longer a "sleeping dragon."

There are three references, in the context of the end-times battles, to a massive eastern power. Revelation 16:12 refers to the "kings of the east" which come over the Euphrates River to do battle in Palestine. In what is believed to be a companion reference, Revelation 9:16 describes the number of the army as 200 million. Daniel 11:44 is undoubtedly another reference to this force which opposes the coming world ruler.

It is significant that the Red Chinese leaders, on several occasions in recent years, have boasted that they could field a "people's army" of 200 million militia. When the Apostle John wrote Revelation some 1,900 years ago, such an army was absolutely unthinkable. Yet here it is—a very real possibility.

More than this, the Chinese have recently completed a highway that could enable them to rapidly reach the Euphrates River. The March 1980 *End Times Digest* states:

> We recently reported that in 1979 China completed the Karakoram Highway from Singkiang province through Pakistan to the Indian Ocean. A spur of

this highway goes through Afghanistan and Iran to Iraq where the Euphrates River runs from Turkey to the Persian Gulf.

And the December 17, 1979, issue of *Aviation Week and Space Technology* reports that the Chinese People's Liberation Army is being trained to launch medium-range ballistic missiles. China is known, of course, to possess nuclear capacity, so she certainly appears capable of taking her place in the end-times scenario sketched by the prophets of long ago.

GOD HAS A PLAN FOR THE ARAB NATIONS

Abraham's son, Ishmael, the forerunner of today's Arab people, received certain promises from God—as recorded in Genesis 16:10-12 and 17:20. God promised that he would be a wild man whose hand would be against every man and every man's hand against him; that he would become fruitful and multiply exceedingly; that he would beget twelve princes; and that he would become a great nation dwelling in the presence of his brethren.

These promises have certainly had at least a partial fulfillment. Salem Kirban, an Arab Christian, proposes in his *Reference Bible* that the twelve "princes" of Ishmael could well be the present day peoples of Lebanon, Syria, Yemen, Jordan, Egypt, Saudi Arabia, Sudan, Libya, Algeria, Tunisia, Morocco and Iraq.

119

These twelve nations today control three million square miles of territory in which is to be found two-thirds of the world's proven oil reserves! Their importance in today's world has already been suggested at the outset of this chapter.

The Arab nations certainly have been "wild"—that is, free and roving and fiercely independent. They have also been against every man, in that they have traditionally been warlike and have experienced much military opposition throughout history.

Isaiah 19:22-25, however, indicates that a day of divine blessing for the Arabs is yet coming. This prophetic utterance (which most scholars agree refers to the period of the 1,000-year reign of Christ) indicates that Egypt, Israel and Syria will worship the Lord *together* in a league that will be a blessing to the nations of earth.

Perhaps the surprising Egyptian-Israeli peace treaty, as well as the amazing world importance of the OPEC nations, are but faint foreshadowings of the fulfillment of these promises from God.

Without question, the sons of Ishmael are a part of the end-time stir that is affecting earth's nations today!

THE RISE OF RUSSIA

Russia is recognized today to be the number one military power in the world. She has achieved this dominion by subterfuge, discipline, self-denial and diabolical dedication to her goal. The Union of Soviet Socialist Republics is committed to total world dominance. Ruthlessly committed. Hungary, East Germany, Czechoslovakia, many African states and Afghanistan are examples of that commitment.

Her position in the world and her role in end-times events was clearly predicted over 2,500 years ago. The prophets Ezekiel, Daniel and Joel wrote about Russia at a time when that land was on the fringe of civilization—a very lightly populated, insignificant nation. They predicted that Russia would play a *major* but (in the light of her lack of power and position at the time the prophecies were written) a *surprising* role in the days that are soon to come upon the world.

Russia's role will be examined in detail in chapter seven—but she has to be at least mentioned here—for she is most definitely one of the nations which is astir as prophecy comes alive!

Not only is the "fig tree nation" of Israel putting forth leaves; the "other trees"—the nations around her—are also doing so. The "summer" of Christ's return must be near!

For Further Reading:
   Daniel: Decoder of Dreams by D. Campbell
   "Solzhenitsyn on Communism" *Time* February 18, 1980.

> "...if the Israelis threaten us, we will wipe
> them out within two days. I can assure you
> our plans are made for this eventuality."
> —Soviet Ambassador Anatoly Dobrymin
> to Henry Kissinger, as related in *The White
> House Years*

> "Thou [Gog] shalt fall upon the mountains
> of Israel—thou and all the people that is
> with thee."
> —Prophet Ezekiel, 2,600 years ago

7

The Bear Pounces—Into a Trap!

Russia is going to invade Israel.

It is not a question of *if*, but *when*.

However, the big Red Bear's pounce upon
tiny Israel will result, not in the annihilation of
the Jews, but rather in the crushing defeat of
the awesome Soviet war machine—a seemingly
unlikely outcome which will create the power
vacuum that precipitates the rise to world power
of earth's final world dictator.

If this sounds like an incredible and
completely impossible scenario, stick around for
the documentation. It's all been foretold by
those "100 percent accurate" prophets, and the
pieces are now starting to fall into place.

First of all, let's look at what the prophet Ezekiel wrote some 2,600 years ago. Chapter 37 of Ezekiel's prophecy contains the account of the valley of dry bones—an army of dead men which had been reduced to dry skeletons, all scattered about. Ezekiel was told by God to preach to the bones and when he did, they began to come together (just like the old Negro spiritual says): sinews and flesh came upon the skeletons, then breath came into them and they stood up—a mighty army.

Then God said to Ezekiel:
Son of man, these bones are the whole house of Israel: behold, they say, Our bones are dried, and our hope is lost: we are cut off for our parts.

Therefore prophesy and say unto them, Thus saith the Lord God; Behold, O my people, I will open your graves, and cause you to come up out of your graves, and bring you into the land of Israel.

And ye shall know that I am the Lord, when I have opened your graves, O my people, and brought you up out of your graves,

And shall put my spirit in you, and ye shall live, and I shall place you in your own land: then shall ye know that I the

124

Lord have spoken it, and performed it, saith the Lord.

The word of the Lord came again unto me, saying,

Moreover, thou son of man, take thee one stick, and write upon it, For Judah, and for the children of Israel his companions: then take another stick, and write upon it, For Joseph, the stock of Ephraim, and for all the house of Israel his companions:

And join them one to another into one stick; and they shall become one in thine hand....

And say unto them, Thus saith the Lord God; Behold, I will take the children of Israel from among the heathen, whither they be gone, and will gather them on every side, and bring them into their own land:

And I will make them one nation in the land upon the mountains of Israel; and one king shall be king to them all: and they shall be no more two nations, neither shall they be divided into two kingdoms any more at all...

And they shall dwell in the land that I have given unto Jacob my servant, wherein your fathers have dwelt; and they shall dwell therein, even they, and their children, and their children's children for ever: and my servant David

shall be their prince for ever.''
                Ezekiel 37:11-17; 21-22; 25

In chapter six I referred to this prophecy in its
fulfillment—as Israel has become once again
one nation...gathered out of over 100 countries.
There can be no doubt that Israel, which as
we'll see in a moment is the target of a military
attack, is the nation in view in this prophecy.

THERE'S MORE TO SEE

But Ezekiel was given a further prophetic
insight, recorded in Ezekiel chapters 38 and 39.
This is such a significant prophetic portion of
Scripture that I urge you to get a Bible and read,
in its entirety, chapters 37, 38 and 39 of Ezekiel.
For convenience, however, I reproduce only
sections of it here.

> And the word of the Lord came unto
> me, saying,
> Son of man, set thy face against Gog,
> the land of Magog, the chief prince of
> Meshech and Tubal, and prophesy
> against him....
> Persia, Ethiopia, and Libya with
> them; all of them with shield and
> helmet:
> Gomer, and all his bands; the house
> of Togarmah of the north quarters, and

all his bands: and many people with thee.

Be thou prepared, and prepare for thyself, thou, and all thy company that are assembled unto thee, and be thou a guard unto them....

Therefore, son of man, prophesy and say unto Gog, Thus saith the Lord God; In that day when my people of Israel dwelleth safely, shalt thou not know it?

And thou shalt come from thy place out of the north parts, thou, and many people with thee, all of them riding upon horses, a great company, and a mighty army:

And thou shalt come up against my people of Israel, as a cloud to cover the land; it shall be in the latter days, and I will bring thee against my land, that the heathen may know me, when I shall be sanctified in thee, O Gog, before their eyes.

Ezekiel 38:1,2,5-7,14-16

For centuries, students of prophecy have believed that the great northern power which leads a confederacy of allies in an attack upon Israel is Russia. For example, in *The Destiny of the Nations*, written in 1864, Dr. John Cummings clearly outlined this view. It was frequently put forward before and since.

What are the reasons for believing that the northern power which leads the attack is Russia? There are at least three.

First, the home location of this leader of the invaders. This is described as the "north quarters" in Ezekiel 38:6,15 and 39:2. The full meaning of the Hebrew word here translated "north" is "uttermost north." There can be only one nation which qualifies as being in the uttermost north of Israel. (By the way, all compass directions in the Bible are given in reference to the Holy Land.) Get a globe. Run a line from Israel to the North Pole. You'll find that it passes through Moscow. Unquestionably all of Russia is to the uttermost north of Israel.

Second, the meaning of the names used in describing this power. These names are "Gog," "Meshech" and "Tubal." (Many scholars point out that the word "Gog" should properly be translated "the prince of Rosh.") Students of languages and their meanings agree that these words refer to Russia, Moscow and Tobolsh. Dr. Merrill Unger in *Beyond the Crystal Ball*, and Hal Lindsey in *The Late Great Planet Earth*, quote famous nineteenth century Hebrew lexicographer William Gesenius as their authority for saying, dogmatically and emphatically, that "Rosh" is to be equated with Russia.

"Meshech" and "Tubal" are identified as the Mushki and the Tubali of the Assyrian records, who over the centuries moved north into the Volga River basin and the region of present day Moscow and Tobolsh. [36]

The third reason for identifying the invaders as being from Russia is their character. Ezekiel's prophecy declares that God says, "Behold, I am against you, O Gog" (Ezekiel 38:3). A statement indicating that God is against *any* people is unusual. He is revealed in the Bible as a God of love, mercy and patience. It almost appears this statement is "out of character" for God. The only obvious reason, then, for God's opposition to Russia has to be her atheism and her overt opposition to God.

The official Soviet position is that God does not exist. Following the teaching of Ludwig Feuerbach in his *Essence of Christianity*, Marx rejected the idea of a God and declared that religion was merely the opiate of the people. The Manifesto plainly states that "Communism abolishes eternal truths, it abolishes all religion and all morality."

"Atheism," wrote Lenin subsequently, "is a natural and inseparable part of Marxism." "We will grapple with the Lord God in due season," said Zinoviev in 1924. "We shall vanquish Him in His highest heaven."

The official program of the Soviet Party, published in 1932, states that one of the party's objectives is "the real emancipation of the working masses from religious prejudices" and that, to this end, it "organizes the widest possible...anti-religious propaganda." Communism denies the existence of God and challenges Him in His highest heaven. [37]

Moreover, Communist U.S.S.R. has undoubtedly done more to destroy faith in God than any other power or ideology in the entire history of the world. In the process, uncounted millions of people, in nation after nation beginning with Russia itself, have been killed in cold blood.

Most serious of all is Russia's treatment of the Jews. God has clearly indicated that Israel is His chosen people and that "I am against them that are against thee." Thus, Russia's cruelty to the Jews—second only to Hitler's—is a powerful reason for the indictment from God, "I am against thee, O Gog."

The leader of the invasion, then, is obviously Russia. Who are her allies?

THE PROPHESIED ALLIES OF RUSSIA

These are listed by Ezekiel as Persia, Ethiopia, Libya, Gomer with all his bands, the house of Togarmah with all his bands, as well as many people (Ezekiel 38:5,6). These nations can be quite definitely identified.

PERSIA. *Persia* is present day *Iran*. In fact, since the 1979 ouster of the Shah and the ending of that 2500-year-old dynasty in the dramatic events currently surrounding that nation, her new Muslim leaders have reverted to the use of that ancient name of Persia.

ETHIOPIA. *Ethiopia* is a translation of the ancient Hebrew word *Cush*, according to Dr. Gesenius. Based on his scholarly conclusions, it is correct to say that the present-day Ethiopians make up a part of the Cushites, though not all of them. Thus, a reasonable view is that Ezekiel's Cush represents a number of present-day north African nations.

Such a conclusion also fits in with the prophecy of Daniel 11 which speaks of the "king of the south"—believed by some scholars to be a description of Cush, or the African-Arab power bloc.

LIBYA. *Libya* is the ancient *Put*. Gesenius' *Hebrew Lexicon* indicates that the descendants of Put became the forefathers of the north African Arab nations such as Libya, Algeria, Morocco and Tunisia. Therefore, the Libya of Ezekiel's prophecy most certainly includes the present day Libya at least, and probably more.

GOMER. *Gomer* and his hordes is evidently *Germany*. Gomer is spoken of in the Jewish Talmud as *Germani*. According to Hal Lindsey in *The Late Great Planet Earth*, the famed Jewish historian Josephus called this people the Rheginians, believed to be found in the area of modern Poland, Czechoslovakia and East

Germany. This conclusion is supported by the Jewish Talmud. Obviously, then, Gomer and his hordes are that part of eastern Europe found behind the Iron Curtain.

TOGARMAH. Many scholars consider *Togermah* to be *Turkey*, or the Turkoman tribes, including perhaps Armenia and the Cossack region of southeastern Russia.[38] There may be other allies as well, since Ezekiel 38:6 makes reference to "many people with thee." But whether there are other nations included or not, it is very clear that Russia provides the leadership and undertakes the preparation of not only herself, but also of her allies for the prophesied invasion of Israel (Ezekiel 38:7).

A DIPLOMATIC PROTEST

According to Ezekiel 38:13, when this Russian invasion occurs, certain maritime commercial nations lodge what may be described as a feeble diplomatic protest. They ask the invaders, "Art thou come to take a spoil?"

Who are these protestors? They are identified as *Sheba* and *Deban* and the merchants of *Tarshish* and all the young lions thereof.

According to Dr. W.F. Albright in the *Bulletin of the American Schools of Oriental Research* published in 1941, Sheba and Deban were land-bound traders located east of Palestine, while Tarshish was the leader of sea traders and marine merchants west of Palestine. The term "Tarshish" came to mean, in time, any land bordering the sea where mining, smelting and trading in metal ore was carried on, says Dr. Nelson Gluech in *The Other Side of Jordan*. Because of this meaning, some commentators have identified Britain as Tarshish and the young lions as her former colonies.

Thus Ezekiel's reference to "Tarshish and its young lions" is believed to be an expression broad enough to take in *all* the younger nations of both the Old and New Worlds. According to Dr. Merrill Unger, this group would evidently include the United States and the Western Alliance, as opposed to the Eastern or Soviet bloc.

WHEN AND WHY
DOES THE ATTACK OCCUR?

Ezekiel's prophecy fixes the time of the Russian confederacy's invasion of Israel at a period which he called "the latter years" or "the latter days"—an era which has witnessed the restoration of the Jews to their land from out of many nations after centuries of dispersion (Ezekiel 36:24; 37:21-22).

More than this, the invasion comes at a time

when the nation is obviously a productive, prosperous land—worthy of an attack to "take a prey, to carry away silver and gold."

The invaded nation is described as dwelling safely, or confidently, in unwalled cities—something which was unheard of in Ezekiel's time, but which of course is common now. More than this, Ezekiel says by way of a reason, *God* will cause Russia to come against Israel—like an animal being dragged by hooks in its jaws (Ezekiel 38:4). Perhaps Russia's drive for world power and the strategic location of the Middle East are the "hooks" God is using.

Now, before we look in detail at the prophesied disastrous outcome of Russia's "pounce," let's consider the current world scene.

THE WAY THINGS ARE SHAPING UP

Israel, as we saw in chapter six, is back in the land and is in fact prospering. The mineral resources of the Dead Sea alone are believed to have a value in the trillions of dollars. The estimate of the value of minerals *other* than phosphates, silicate sand, copper, manganese, iron and feldspar is $5,673,987,000,000 according to the 1975 *Economic Bulletin of Israel*, Vol. 5, No. 3. [39]

She *is* dwelling in unwalled cities—if not safely, at least *confidently*, which some feel is a more accurate rendering of the word translated "safely" in Ezekiel's prophecy.

Russia, which at the time of Ezekiel's prophecy was out on the fringes of civilization with a tiny, insignificant population, is today a monstrous superpower on the march to global domination. Since the end of World War I, when the Communists overthrew the Czar and set out on the road to world conquest, the U.S.S.R. has had an incredible rise to awesome might on a global scale.

The nation that twelve years before the Communist Revolution was actually beaten by little Japan in the Russo-Japanese War of 1905 is now the rampaging Red Bear—feared by all the world—with more than a third of the earth's population today living under Communism as a result of her 65-year campaign of intrigue, revolution and outright war.

Now, although debate related to the SALT II talks continues to rage over the question of military superiority, it is apparent that Russia has become the world's number one military power, having overcome a two-to-one U.S. lead in strategic nuclear forces during the 70s. A comparison of the most advanced missiles of each nation (*Time*, May 1979) shows that the Soviet's SS-18 is able to deliver *ten times* the kiloton force of America's top ICBM, the Minuteman III. And the SS-18s (a terrifying weapon against which no defence currently exists) outnumber Minutemen by a wide margin.[40]

It is also apparent that Russia is developing chemical weaponry. The September 1979 *Reader's Digest* reported that the Red Army includes a chemical-warfare contingent of 80-100,000 men. The article gives a frightening overview of the chemical warfare capacity being developed by the Soviets.[41] More than this, the October 29, 1979, issue of *Aviation Week and Space Technology* claimed that, for the most recent full year for which figures were available, the U.S.S.R. outstripped the U.S. in military expenditures by $39 billion![42] The June 29, 1980, issue of *The Don Bell Report* claims that

> ...according to Major General George Keegan, former Air Force Chief of Intelligence, the Soviet Union now has the following advantages over the United States and its European allies: A 6 to 1 advantage in nuclear firepower expressed in megatonnage; a 47 to 1 weapons advantage in defense against nuclear attack; a 5 to 1 advantage in tanks; a 7 to 1 advantage in artillery; a 100 to 1 advantage in regular ammunition; a 10 to 1 advantage in fighter bombers; a 5 to 1 advantage in all classes of navy ships; a 3 to 1

advantage in nuclear powered attack submarines; and so on. [43]

The *US News and World Report* (October 30, 1978) declared, "By 1983, most analysts predict Russia will achieve an unprecedented, but probably temporary, strategic advantage over the U.S.....Very roughly it would appear that the optimal period of Soviet security policy will be the next five years or so.... In this situation, strategic analysts warn, the Soviets will be tempted to exploit their military advantage before the U.S. can reverse the balance." [44]

On May 11-13, 1980, an ABC three-part TV special entitled "Democracy's Arsenal is Empty" painted a bleak picture of the U.S. capacity to do global battle. Declaring that the States now has only a 60-90 day weaponry supply, and that it would take months to turn industry around for the massive production of adequate armaments, the documentary claimed that a time lag of two years (from a decision to rearm to implementation) is a minimum. Even to get the present "obsolete" armed forces into proper fighting trim would take months, according to the special.

In contrast, the program claimed that the Soviet war machine is delivering a new modernized aircraft every nineteen hours, and that the significant U.S.S.R. military superiority over the U.S. is not only unquestioned, but growing. [45] And the Soviets are developing their allies for this prophesied invasion.

In an excellent documentary entitled *The Dominoes are Falling*, Charles Pack checks off the entry of various nations into the Russian confederacy. The first to be taken into the ranks was *East Germany* (*Gomer*)—at the close of World War II.[46] The next was *Libya*, which in 1969 had a pro-Communist coup, signalling a sharp turn from ties with the U.S. to strong involvement in the Russia orbit under the present leadership of leftist strongman Premier Quaddafi. (Subsequently, in the early 70s, the USAF had to move out of Wheelers base.) The June 1978 *Reader's Digest* documented the Soviet drive in all of north Africa in an article entitled ''Russia's Ruthless Reach into Africa.''[47]

Ethiopia was the next. Emperor Selassie, the 77-year-old pro-West ruler, was deposed by a pro-Communist coup and died in 1976. Then in 1977, although the U.S. had poured $637 million aid into Ethiopia over 30 years, the Marxists gave American officials and their families, 300 in all, four days in which to get out. At the same time, shipments of Soviet weapons began arriving in Ethiopia—followed by Soviet ''advisors.''[48]

RED INTRIGUE. Then came *Persia*, or *Iran*. This nation has figured most prominently in world news in recent months—with the January

1979 ouster of the pro-Western Shah and the very definite turn toward the Communist orbit, in spite of the Ayatollah Khomeini's strong Muslim stance.

It is most interesting to note that Russia has a 1921 treaty with Iran—to protect her from invasion, instability or other incident affecting the security of both countries. After what has happened in Afghanistan in December 1979, with the Russian invasion on the pretext of a call for help, it would not be difficult to envision a Russian move, if necessary from the Soviet point of view, into Iran. [49]

U.S. News & World Report, on November 26, 1979, says that "on October 24, two days after Shah Mohammad Reza Pahlevi was admitted to a New York Hospital and eleven days before Iranian mobs seized the embassy, Radio Moscow beamed this message in Persian to Iran: "Collaboration between the Shah and the U.S. would threaten the Republic in Iran." The warning echoed the words of Ayatollah Ruhollah Khomeini.

The article continues:

Four days before the takeover, Radio Moscow's commentator Vera Bodeva declared in a "Dear Friends" message in Persian: "We are witnessing fresh, dangerous plots and intrigues against the Iranian Republic.... The people of Iran who are experienced in revolutionary struggles...are well able to stop the intrigues of imperialism and reaction and to defend what they gained from their revolution.... Great significance attaches to the slogan 'Death to U.S. Imperialism.' "

Immediately after the takeover, the National Voice of Iran, broadcasting from Soviet soil, charged that the U.S. Embassy was the "center of corruption and anti-Iranian conspiracies."

Added a Persian-language broadcast from Radio Moscow: "The anger of the Iranian nation and its youth who ask that a stop be put to U.S. imperialist interference in the country's affairs is totally understandable and logical." [50]

A Russian invasion of Iran may not be necessary.

In his February 1980 *Report*, James Sinclair of New York details the procedure by which the Communists manipulated the Iranian crisis—first with overtures to the Shah in the 60s; then technical aid; followed by 4,000 technical advisors, all of whom spoke the Iranian language; and then an Iranian-based transmitter to broadcast Communist propaganda, at the same time massing troops on the border in a psychological move.

Too late, the Shah (whose character or rule is not being defended or even debated here) recognized the threat. Shortly after his deposal, he asked why the West could not understand that the Communists were manipulating the uprising. He said, "Very few of the young people parading behind Khomeini's picture have ever set foot in a mosque"—a view with which the CIA concurs.[51] The February 18, 1980, *Time* article by Solzhenitsyn on Communism, which clearly spells out Communism's undeviating goal of world domination, supports this contention.[52]

AND MORE INTRIGUE. James Sinclair maintains that *Turkey*, the fifth and last of the nations listed individually by name in Ezekiel, is going the route of Iran. Since 1950, Turkey has been a member of NATO—the Western defence alliance. In 1978, for the first time in 45 years, a Soviet senior military official went to Turkey to discuss the Turkish military situation. A transmitter for the recently-legalized Communist party in Turkey has been constructed. The Soviets are now giving more aid to Turkey than to any other developing or western nation.

Several huge joint technical projects—involving numerous Turkish-speaking Soviet advisors—are under way. Soviet troops are massed on the border. Increasingly, leftist workers have been involved in bloody rioting. Unemployment is high and the nation is in deep turmoil.[53]

This sort of chaos is made-to-order for a Soviet takover. It is the basic formula which has been used in Russia's domination of dozens of countries. Perhaps by the time this is in print, Turkey will have gone the way of Iran or Afghanistan. Whether that is so or not, it is certain that at some time Turkey will become an ally of Russia against Israel, for God has foretold it.

SUMMING IT ALL UP

In summary, then, we have Israel in the land; we have a powerful northern nation, Russia (with the prophesied allies already in her camp or rapidly moving that way); and we see the Red Bear making moves and threatening noises against Israel.

It is significant to note that Yassar Arafat, head of the Palestinian Liberation Organization, has frequently held "successful" talks with the Soviets' highest-ranking leaders (including Brezhnev). Recently the Soviets and the PLO issued a joint statement calling for "closer ties between Moscow and *all* elements of the PLO."

This is noteworthy when the goal of the PLO is recalled. Arafat declares, "We don't recognize Israel. Israel is still absorbing and usurping a part of *our* country." He has pledged his guerrillas to "fight unto death to liberate Palestine.... Palestine can be restored only by blood, by the gun." He continues, "We insist on a 100 percent independent Palestinian state on every yard of Palestinian soil freed from Israel by military action or diplomacy." The charter of the PLO calls for "dismantling the Jewish state and replacing it with a non-sectarian Palestinian nation." (Above quotations from various issues of the *Los Angeles Times*.) [54]

And Russia, obviously, fully supports the PLO in this goal.

EGYPT—THE AMAZING ABSENTEE IN THE LINEUP AGAINST ISRAEL

Surprisingly, Egypt—*the one nation which, until recently, you would certainly have expected to find in the lineup against Israel*—is not mentioned in Ezekiel's prophecy! For years students of prophecy puzzled over this fact. They concluded that Egypt—a long-term enemy of Israel—must be included in the phrase "and many people with thee." But that was not too satisfactory an explanation because of Egypt's importance in the biblical record.

It is true that Egypt and Israel *have* been traditional and important enemies from ancient times. Since the 1948 statehood of Israel, the two nations have been antagonists to some degree in each of the four bitter wars fought in the Middle East.

In addition, for years and at a staggering cost, Russia (the future invader) has cultivated Egyptian friendship and support. But in the mid-to-late 70s, Egyptian President Sadat downplayed Russian influence, sent the Soviet advisors home and began to steer an independent course.

Then on March 26, 1979, the totally improbable happened: *Israel and Egypt signed a peace treaty!*

I was in New York City for a committee meeting on that historic day. The major New York dailies were on strike, but I picked up a suburban newspaper—its front page displaying a huge full-color photo of Egyptian President Sadat, Israeli Prime Minister Begin and U.S. President Carter signing the treaty on the lawn of the White House. A prophecy from the book of Isaiah and the enormous headline "Let There Be No More Bloodshed" dominated almost the entire page. [55]

I was electrified by the event! Against all odds, the peace treaty had been signed! And in spite of huge problems, the major one being the Palestinian refugee question, agreement is slowly being worked out.

The *Jerusalem Post* details in its daily news stories the progress which is steadily being made toward the normalization of relations between the two former enemies: border openings, the return of sections of the Sinai to Egypt, exchanges of official visits, a telephone link, mail service—dozens of big and little, but important, steps toward friendship. [56] And all of this is occurring in the face of bitter attacks and sanctions against Egypt by other Arab nations who regard her as a traitor.

It's interesting, is it not, that Ezekiel left Egypt out of the lineup that accompanies Russia in her invasion of Israel? Very interesting—in light of the fact that within the past seven years, Egypt has reversed the attitude of the ages, the trend of current Communist involvement and risked the animosity of her Arab brothers in order to become a peaceful neighbor of Israel.

Though I recognize that the peace treaty may not be fully ratified and that the situation could change, still allowing Egypt to be one of the "many with thee" in Ezekiel, I do not think it will happen. I believe the Egypt-Israeli peace treaty is a fulfillment of prophecy.

Thus—the lineup of the invaders, with its inclusions and omissions, appears to be nearing completion.

WHEN WILL THE ATTACK COME?

There are differing opinions among students of prophecy as to exactly when this invasion will occur. I personally do not believe that it is possible to be dogmatic about the exact time, though I will outline my considered opinion.

Some believe that the invasion will come

three and one-half years into the seven-year period known as the Great Tribulation, that time of terrible suffering for the Jews and of the pouring out of God's wrath upon a godless earth. The Church will have already been taken out of the earth in the Rapture, as described briefly in chapter three.

Others hold that it will occur at the very outset of that seven-year time block, while still others believe that it will come up to three and one-half years before the Great Tribulation, the beginning of which is marked by a peace treaty between Israel and the coming world dictator (called the Antichrist), whom we'll consider in chapter eight.

My own view is that the invasion will occur shortly after the Rapture, near the time the Antichrist makes his seven-year treaty with Israel—though I agree it could possibly be as early as three and one-half years before.

(The reason for the flexibility is Ezekiel's prophesy that "they who dwell in the cities of Israel" would burn as fuel for seven years the discarded weapons of the war. Some believe that the war must then occur three and one-half years before the treaty since, as we shall see, the Antichrist breaks the treaty with Israel after three and one-half years and begins all-out persecution of the Jews, causing them to flee the land. Thus for them to have seven years in which to burn weapons puts the invasion back to three and one-half years prior to the treaty.

However, Ezekiel does not say that the *Jews* will burn the weapons for seven years but simply that *they that dwell in the cities of Israel* will do so—and these could be other than Jews.)

Now, I don't believe it is possible nor necessary to be dogmatic on this point. One reason why I feel that the invasion will come shortly *after* the Rapture is that the Rapture itself may—through the mysterious disappearance of large numbers of people (particularly in the West) and the resultant confusion—actually trigger the attack.

It will certainly come after the ten-nation revived Roman Empire is assembled. The Antichrist will already be on the world stage or right in the wings, just awaiting the right moment to take charge of that confederacy in the way God has revealed he will, stepping into the power vacuum created by the defeat of the Russian power bloc in Israel.

WHAT WILL HAPPEN?

Again, it is not possible to be dogmatic about every move or the exact sequence of events, inasmuch as differing views are held by competent scholars. However, this could be the scenario—taking into account both Ezekiel's prophecy and that of Daniel in chapter 11: Sometime after the Antichrist, head of the ten-nation confederacy, signs a seven-year treaty with Israel, the king of the south—the Arab bloc—will invade Israel (Daniel 11:40).* At this point, the entire Russian confederacy will come down upon the Jews like a whirlwind—with chariots, horsemen and many ships.† Apparently the Russians will double-cross the Arabs, for Daniel 11:40-43 indicates that their hordes will enter not only Israel, but many countries—with Egypt, Libya and Ethiopia specifically singled out as being taken. This fits the apparent desire of the Soviets to control the entire Middle East because of its oil.

It is at this juncture that the nations (which we have already indicated could be the NATO powers) utter their feeble protest, to which Russia, the superpower, pays no attention whatever (Ezekiel 38:18).

(Unfortunately, this seems to be the way things are. Since Vietnam and all of the massive protests over that tragic involvement, the U.S.

---

* Daniel 11:36-40 refers to the Antichrist. However, verse 40 introduces the "king of the north" (Russia) who, grammatically, **must** remain the subject for the rest of the chapter.

† Whether this reference to chariots and horses is to be taken literally or is merely a description of military might is the subject of some debate among prophetic students. I tend to feel that it is the latter, but would not rule out the possibility of the use of horses, with which Russia is extremely well supplied.

has been unwilling and/or unable to undertake any sort of military response. The Afghanistan invasion is an example of this inability. Many commentators feel that Afghanistan was in fact a test of the U.S. resolve to resist...and that there is no longer any such resolve. This fits prophetically, sad to say, for it is tragic to see American influence steadily declining.)

At this point, the tidings from the north (the north of Africa) where the king of the north is at this moment in the prophetic preview, and from the east (the European Common Market and the Oriental armies) cause the principal invader to set up headquarters in Israel. Here, upon the mountains of Israel, Russia's war machine is destroyed.

AN AMAZING OUTCOME

Daniel says simply that "he shall come to his end—and none shall help him." The Russian army *is not defeated in battle*. Ezekiel says that *God* will destroy Russia's armies. Here's his prophecy:

> Thus saith the Lord God; Behold, I am against thee, O Gog.
> And I will turn thee back, and leave but the sixth part of thee, and will cause thee to come up from the north parts, and will bring thee upon the mountains of Israel:

149

And I will smite thy bow out of thy left hand, and will cause thine arrows to fall out of thy right hand.

Thou shalt fall upon the mountains of Israel, thou, and all thy bands, and the people that is with thee: I will give thee unto the ravenous birds of every sort, and to the beasts of the field to be devoured.

Thou shalt fall upon the open field: for I have spoken it, saith the Lord God.

And I will send a fire on Magog, and among them that dwell carelessly in the isles: and they shall know that I am the Lord.

So will I make my holy name known in the midst of my people Israel; and I will not let them pollute my holy name any more: and the heathen shall know that I am the Lord, the Holy One in Israel.

Ezekiel 39:2-7

Apparently *unusual natural disasters* like earthquake and upheaval, pestilence, torrential rain and hailstones combined with *supernatural* fire, brimstone and the outbreak of vicious *fighting among the invaders themselves* will result in the destruction of five-sixths of the entire Soviet military force.

In addition, God says He will rain fire upon Magog (Russia itself) and on those who dwell in the coastlands. Some have speculated that this refers to nuclear destruction. It could indeed, but whether this is so or not, one fact is very clear: all the world will realize that the destruction of the Russian confederacy was the work of God—not man.

A good deal of discussion has arisen over the description here of the kind of weaponry described, particularly over the burning of the discarded weapons of the invaders as fuel. Skeptics have had a field day with this, pointing out that steel doesn't burn. Others have suggested it describes a yet-to-be-developed nuclear fission potential.

In recent years, there have been numerous reports circulated of a substance called "lignostone"—said to have been developed in Ter Apel, Holland, in the mid-1960s. According to such reports, lignostone is a chemically treated wood which is very lightweight but which, like steel, can be used for armor plating. It reportedly burns more readily and intensely than coal. Moreover, the Russians are said to be the principal producers and users of it.

All of this fits the prophetic picture extremely well—except that I have been completely unable to confirm the existence of such a substance. Extensive research at several university libraries failed to turn up even so much as the mention of the name in *anything*—dictionaries, technical journals or scientific bulletins. This does not prove its

151

non-existence, of course, but it does appear that the story is unfounded.

However, whatever the reference to burning the weapons means need not be fully understood inasmuch as numerous developments in recent years have made understandable and convincing, even to skeptics, prophecies which were once said to be ridiculous.

The culmination of these events can't be too far away—given the rapidity with which the pieces are falling into place. Obviously, Russia's leaders are either totally unaware of what God's Word says—or, more likely, just do not believe it, as they press forward to the day when they will be brought down upon Israel—like an animal being led by a hook in its jaws!

Unquestionably, their invasion *will* occur and the fact that it appears to be looming so near should cause all thoughtful persons to be ready for the Rapture.

"And the king shall do according to his will; and he shall exalt himself, and magnify himself above every god...for he shall magnify himself above all."

Prophet Daniel in Babylon

"Let him that hath understanding count the number of the beast: for it is the number of a man; and his number is six, six, six!"

Prophet John on Patmos

8

The Coming World Dictator

I went shopping with my wife, Joyce, recently. For a change of pace, we drove over to the nearby city of Langley, B.C., which boasts a new Safeway store—said (at the time of this writing) to be Canada's most modern supermarket. Upon going through at the shiny new computerized checkouts, we were handed a descriptive newssheet titled "This Canada Safeway Store is equipped with Electronic Scanners to utilize the UPC."

The interesting and informative brochure described in some detail the spaceage computerized technology entailed in utilizing the Universal Product Code—that vertical arrangement of thick and thin bars now appearing on the majority of products throughout North America. Checking out now is accompanied by a swift series of beeps as the UPC is swept over a scanner. A detailed printout is instantly prepared.

This technological advance, which promises to become commonplace, is believed to be a forerunner and key factor in the fulfillment of certain extremely significant prophecies involving the coming world dictator—better known as the Antichrist. Let me explain after we've looked at the prophetic record.

The prophets foretold the appearance, at the end time, of a counterfeit Christ—an amazing man energized, given over to and controlled by Satan, with enormous power over all who live upon the earth. The Scriptures indicate that only those who swear allegiance to this dictator by wearing his mark either in their foreheads or on their right hands will be permitted to buy or sell. In other words, he will have life or death power over all people on earth.

A few years ago this prospect was viewed by skeptics as a virtual impossibility. Today, however, as the computer increasingly affects everyone's way of life, the cashless society becomes ever more a possibility while the drive for a one-world government subtly continues, that which seemed impossible is now very much an eventuality.

Let's carefully check out the composite prophetic portrayal of this coming leader before we see how current world conditions fit that picture.

The Antichrist first appears in Daniel's prophecy. You will recall the vision in which Daniel saw four strange beasts, symbolizing four successive world empires. The fourth beast had, as well as iron teeth and bronze claws, ten horns (Daniel 7:7-28). From these grew an additional "little horn" which took over three others and "made war with the saints." Daniel described this horn in detail:

> And the ten horns out of this kingdom are ten kings that shall arise: and another shall rise after them; and he shall be diverse from the first, and he shall subdue three kings.
>
> And he shall speak great words against the most High, and shall wear out the saints of the most High, and think to change times and laws: and they shall be given into his hand until a time and times and the dividing of time.
>
> But the judgment shall sit, and they shall take away his dominion, to consume and to destroy it unto the end.
>
> And the kingdom and dominion, and the greatness of the kingdom under the whole heaven, shall be given to the people of the saints of the most High, whose kingdom is an everlasting kingdom, and all dominions shall serve

and obey him.

Daniel 7:24-27

From this we understand that earth's coming final ruler arises out of the revived Roman Empire, probably from one of the lesser nations (a "little horn"). He subdues three of the other ten nations and becomes supreme over the ten. He is a blasphemer against God, a persecutor of the saints, and one who will adjust laws to his will and advantage—a dictator whose days, however, are numbered.

JESUS SPEAKS

Jesus, in Matthew 24:15,21, made reference to other prophecies from Daniel (4:27; 11:31; 12:11) relating to this future "Fuhrer." Here, Christ spoke of "an abomination that causes desolation" which will arise and create sorrow unequalled in the past or future of God's people.

That prophecy was partially fulfilled in A.D. 70 when the Roman armies destroyed the Temple, which has never been rebuilt to this day. But you'll recall that prophecies often have a double reference. Obviously this one has, for when Jesus added in Matthew 24:22 that "if the Lord had not cut short those days, no one would survive, but for the sake of the elect—He has shortened them," He was saying something which could only apply to the Tribulation at the end of the age.

From these prophecies we understand that the Antichrist will make a treaty with Israel for one "week" of years—that is, seven years. Under that treaty, sacrifices will quite obviously be reinstated in a temple in Jerusalem, but halfway through the week of years, or at the three and one-half year point, the Antichrist will cause the sacrifices to end and an abomination to be put in their place.

PAUL PROPHESIES

More information on the appearance and rule of the Antichrist comes through the Apostle Paul in his second letter to the Thessalonians. In Paul's first letter to the believers at Thessalonica, he had written about the Lord's return to earth to take both dead and living saints to Himself (I Thessalonians 4:13-18). However, this wonderful message of hope had confused the Christians there, for in the light of the difficult times they were undergoing, many of them concluded that they had missed that return and were already in the "day of the Lord"—the period of great tribulation.

Paul very quickly and forcefully set that straight by writing, "Let no man deceive you by any means: for that day shall not come except there come a falling away first, and that man of sin be revealed, the son of perdition'' (2:3).

Then he went on to describe that ''man of sin.'' This coming ruler will oppose God, seek to exalt himself above God and even declare that he is God. To do so, the man of sin will take his place in the temple and outlaw any worship not directed to him. He is empowered by Satan to perform all kinds of counterfeit miracles, signs and wonders, deceiving those who are perishing.

The entire personality and mission of the Antichrist is characterized by rebellion against God. The Greek word translated ''falling away'' in 2:3 is *apostasia*, which can also mean ''rebellion'' or ''revolt.''

Now it is true that since the fall of mankind back in the Garden of Eden, humanity, apart from Jesus Christ, has been in a state of rebellion against God. This spirit of lawlessness, says Paul, is already at work (2:7). In and under the Antichrist, however, that rebellion will blossom into a deliberate, defiant, generalized, all-encompassing rejection of God and Christ. In the meantime, it is being restrained, or held back, by what Paul calls the ''restrainer'' in 2:7.*

---

* In the language of the King James Version, the restrainer is described as ''he who now letteth.'' ''Let'' is to be understood as meaning to **hinder**, or **prevent** in this archaic usage.

The restrainer is obviously the Holy Spirit in the midst of His people, the Church. In that sense He will be removed when Jesus snatches the Church away. This does not mean that the Holy Spirit will be absent from the earth. No—He will be present as He was during the Old Testament period before the birth of the Church. But in His restraining-of-evil work in and through the Church (that body of believers all around the world in whom He dwells) He will be removed at the Rapture.

And then the rebellion will spread rapidly, until it is full-blown under the Antichrist, who will be its embodiment.

JOHN JOINS IN

Finally, John, in one of his letters and in the Revelation, adds several more details on this coming evil one. In I John 2:18-27 John refers to the Antichrist. The Greek prefix translated "anti" in this portion has two meanings. One of these is *against* and the other *instead of*. So we see that the Antichrist is not just against Christ but plans to be instead of Him.

The book of the Revelation describes the apocalypse. John writes that judgments of God upon the earth will be detailed in a scroll with seven seals, each seal containing judgments. When the seventh seal is opened, seven trumpets are blown—each marking a further judgment upon the earth.

In turn, the seventh trumpet will introduce the seven vial, or bowl, judgments—the worst part of the Tribulation.

In that context, John prophetically describes the Antichrist as well as his *counterfeit* Holy Spirit—the evil false prophet (Revelation 13). The nefarious activity, final struggle and doom of these evil personages is foretold in Revelation 19:11-21.

The Antichrist is awesome. He is empowered by Satan. He blasphemes God. He apparently rises from the dead, or at least from what would be considered a fatal wound. He takes control of the world through unprecedented political authority and is worshipped by all except the saints of God. He appears to be invincible.

While the Antichrist obviously handles political matters, the false prophet is in charge of religious affairs. It will evidently be a very religious time, in which the false prophet performs miracles to win people to the worship of the Dictator. (One miracle involves causing the statue of the Antichrist to apparently come to life.)

Failing persuasion, there is always economic coercion—with no one permitted to buy or sell unless he/she receives the mark of the Antichrist in either forehead or hand. John declares that the mark is a number—666. Few portions of Scripture have triggered more speculation, since in Hebrew and Greek each letter has a numerical value. Intriguingly enough, the total of those values in the Antichrist's name comes to 666. All kinds of formulas have been unsuccessfully used through the years to "prove" that this person or that is the Antichrist!

John goes on to describe how God's wrath is poured out on all who do receive the beast's mark. In response, the arrogant, satanic Antichrist will rise against God and seek to destroy God's people, especially the 144,000 Jewish evangelists who will have become a feature of this period. This will result in a gathering of the armies of earth to Palestine for Armageddon, which we'll consider in detail in chapter twelve.

The sequel to this fearsome conflict will be the appearance from heaven of the Lord Jesus Christ and His armies. The Antichrist and false prophet will be taken and cast into the lake of fire, and all the rest of his cohorts will be slain (Revelation 19:11-21).

WHAT DOES THE CURRENT SCENE LOOK LIKE?

Now, are there indications in our world today that lead us to believe we could be near to the kind of situation under the Antichrist foretold by these prophets?

Indeed there are.

We suggested that the ultramodern Safeway

we visited with its UPC checkout facilities is a hint of global preparation, albeit unwittingly, for a world dictator.

Far more sophisticated computerized stores exist elsewhere, particularly in the U.S. and Japan. For example, "the world's first fully automated supermarket," the OK Supermarket in Kokubunji, Japan, has since its opening in 1975 "all but eliminated shoplifting, employee pilfering and cashier mistakes," according to *Newsweek*. Such a store is most definitely the wave of the future. [57]

And what a future the technicians foresee! The computer—a technical wonder that has the ability to dictate that every man, woman and child in the world lives, works, buys and sells under a system of code marks and numbers—is coming of age. Consider this scenario of the future involving Mr. and Mrs. Jones, your average citizens.

MEET THE JONESES

By means of a touch-tone telephone as the link between his company computer and the area's central computer (CENCOM for short), Mr. Jones's earnings are automatically electronically deposited for him in his computerized, nationalized bank account. No waiting for a paycheck on the first and fifteenth. No traffic hassle on the way to the bank. No bank deposit lineups. No bother either with the payment of recurring bills like water, gas, light, telephone, insurance, car or mortgage. All these are handled routinely by CENCOM. At month's end, Mr. Jones gets a detailed statement showing dates and earnings deposited, deductions, payments and balance.

When Mrs. Jones goes shopping, she takes with her a plastic identification card—bearing a black magnetic strip containing electronic bits of information about her. The information is not visible to the human eye, insuring privacy.

In order to get into the store, which is locked and secured by the electronic surveillance of CENCOM, Mrs. Jones must insert the card into a "reader slot," at the same time entering her private, government-issued ID number into the computer. If the two match, her cards are released and she is allowed to enter the store. The same procedure must be followed to get out. [58]

Instead of picking items from shelves, Mrs. Jones looks at merchandise through windows and selects what she wants by pushing a button. Her CENCOM card in a slot releases the merchandise.

When she has completed her selections and is at the checkout, she again produces her card, enters her ID number and has her groceries with their UPC passed over a laser scanner which flashes information about them on a viewing screen on the ECR (electronic cash register) while it also records the transaction. When all purchases have been recorded, the "total" button is pressed and the sum is checked automatically by CENCOM against the Jones family bank account. If enough "buying rights" (funds) are there to cover the purchase, CENCOM authorizes the sale, automatically takes the amount from the Jones account and transfers it electronically to the store's account.

A similar transaction occurs at the gas station or soft drink machine or any other store.

No money ever changes hands!

What a deterrent to crime! —a plus which will certainly be used to sell the concept to the public.

Another ostensible benefit is that CENCOM can carefully control credit and debt. Knowing that Mr. Jones gets paid once every fourteen days, CENCOM keeps the family solvent by dividing those earnings by fourteen to come up with the daily allotment of "buying rights" available. CENCOM can be programmed to release only that amount each day.

IT'S ALREADY IN USE

Sound fantastic? Too futuristic to be feasible?

There are a large number of the elements in the above scenario which are *already* in effect in various parts of the world. Since 1967, the 1,300 plus employees of the Sarasota, Florida,

Memorial Hospital have been on a "checkless" payroll system keyed by a Honeywell 1259 computer tied into fourteen area banks. This arrangement is in widespread use in the United States, with checkless handling of military personnel and Social Security recipients, with similar handling of the entire civil service payroll envisioned in the near future.[59]

In Holland, over 90 percent of mortgage and rental payments are handled cashlessly.

Back in 1975, Thomas G. Waage, senior Vice-President of the New York Branch of the Federal Reserve Bank, said in a UPI release that a new electronic system of exchange *had* to be developed or the U.S. banking system would "choke" under an avalanche of checks. He said that a cashless society could be reached in ten years time should there be a serious decision by everyone to implement it.[60]

A number of pilot projects have been run. Universal Product Coding and laser scanning is growing, and now automated banking is under way. The *New York Times* in April 1975 reported that "what is happening in banking now is an electronic revolution in the transfer of money on the wholesale level which is beginning to be felt at the retail level."[61]

IT'S GOING TO BE SWIFT!

The January 1975 issue of *Burroughs*

Clearing House magazine carried an article which shows that EFT (Electronic Fund Transfer) has gone international. The opening paragraphs read in part:

> Burroughs Corp. has been selected by the Society for Worldwide Interbank Financial Telecommunications (S.W.I.F.T.) to supply data processing and data communications equipment which will be used in a *new international telecommunications network*. S.W.I.F.T., which is based in Brussels, currently has a membership of 246 banks with a private communications system for the transmission of payment and other messages associated with international banking. Initially, the S.W.I.F.T. network will be comprised of switching Burroughs data concentrators in Amsterdam, Brussels, Copenhagen, Frankfurt, Helsinki, London, Milan, Montreal, New York, Oslo, Paris, Stockholm, Vienna and Zurich. The data concentrators in each country will be connected to terminals in member banks in that country. Most messages transmitted on the S.W.I.F.T. network will be delivered anywhere in the system within a minute of being entered.[62]

As reported in *Moneysworth* magazine in

May 1975, the U.S. federal courts ruled to permit banks to install EFT terminals in stores, public buildings, stadiums and even street corners. [63]

Touch Tone telephones can and are being used to initiate financial transactions. It is not difficult to see how such a system could be used to control the lives of people. One author in the U.S. states that Federal planners foresee the day when every citizen has a "money card" instead of money—electronically connected to the Federal Reserve Bank. The accounts of tax offenders or political mavericks could be automatically closed—in which case a red light triggered at the point of purchase would prevent the shopkeeper from selling anything to the offender. [64]

In an Associated Press release dated August 18, 1975, which appeared in newspapers all over the U.S., Democratic Senator Frank Church, chairman of a committee then investigating U.S. intelligence activities, was quoted as saying that "the government has the technological capacity to impose 'total tyranny' if ever a dictator came to power. There would be no place to hide." [65]

Admittedly such a total changeover of the magnitude envisioned above would create enormous problems and adjustments. There would undoubtedly be a great deal of resistance. Journalists, speakers and authors voice grave concerns about the danger of totalitarian control. Robert Ellis Smith in his book *PRIVACY: How to Protect What's Left of It* focuses on ways to fight the growing control by government.

However, Wally Wood Jr., in an excellent, extremely well-documented book, *Cashless Society: A World Without Money*, points out that the kind of dramatic change envisioned above may be forced upon the world through financial crisis.

And there can be little question that the world is moving into an era of crisis and change. We're told that a "new economic order looms." Willard Cantelon in two documentary-style books, *The Day the Dollar Dies* and *World Without Money*, paints a chilling picture of coming events.

The December 1979 issue of *Canadian Business* magazine carried a lengthy forecast feature entitled "The Unpredictable Decade — the 1980s." In it the editors admitted that nobody can say with absolute certainty what the economy is going to do — other than (to quote J.P. Morgan about the market) "fluctuate."

The consensus among the experts, the editors reported, was that "all of them hope the worst will not happen, and most of them fear that it will."

"The worst envisioned would be a global monetary collapse, triggered by energy shortages, and characterized by uncontrolled, Weimar-style inflation that wipes out paper assets, beggars the middle class and impoverishes everyone but the speculators.''[66]

At the very least, says A.F. Hudson, an international consultant on precious metals and currency markets for Mead and Co. Ltd. in Montreal, we're in for a fundamental restructuring of the global monetary system, with the European Common Market emerging as the strongest currency bloc—probably backed by gold.

When, then, can we expect the depression? According to Hudson, ''The realization at street level will be felt in 1983—that will be the moment of no return, exactly 1983—when the service charge on the US debt will equal the country's net capital-generating capacity, about $100 billion in 1982-83. That will be the day when private investment is limited to replacing worn-out capital goods. That is the day when the US, with its medical care, unemployment insurance and other social programs (which for political reasons it will be unable to abandon), will be incapable of financing the interest rate on its debt through any further borrowing.

''An important point to understand is that it will be a hyperinflationary depression—and we already entered an inflationary depression in 1973. The consequences will be enormous on a global scale."[67]

Certainly, because of the potential chaos, the sort of electronic fund surveillance we have briefly described could be instituted quite quickly, many experts fear. The purpose of this chapter is not to demonstrate exactly how this can and will be done, but to show that it quite conceivably *could* be.

HOW ABOUT A MARK?

Only one further step would then need to be taken to fit perfectly the prophesied control of the coming Antichrist. That would be quite simply to mark people's hands or foreheads with his code which would authorize them to buy or sell.

The idea has been seriously proposed. The September 20, 1973, *Senior Scholastics* magazine suggested, in an article titled "Public Needs and Private Rights—Who is Watching You?":

All buying and selling in the program will be done by computer. No currency, no change, no checks. In the program, people would receive a number that had been assigned them tattooed in their

170

wrist or forehead. The number is put on
by a laser beam and cannot be felt. The
number in the body is not seen with the
naked eye and is as permanent as your
fingerprints. All items of consumer
goods will be marked with a computer
mark. The computer outlet in the store
which picks up the number on the items
at the check stand will also pick up the
number in the person's body and
automatically total the price and deduct
the amount from the person's "Special
Drawing Rights" account.... [68]

The use of laser branding is already a reality.
In one of the best-documented books I've ever
seen, Ron Steele demonstrates convincingly
that the technology to mark, register and keep
tabs on people is here. Indeed, such marking is
now in widespread use with pets and livestock.
Through laser branding and a universal,
unalterable mark developed by Dr. R. Keith
Farell of Washington State University, *every
animal in the world could be individually
identified*.

"It is quick and painless," says its developer,
Dr. Farell. In a fraction of a second a technician
can stitch a brand or initial. "And it is
theoretically possible to include man as another
one of these animals," says the doctor, who
admits he has branded himself in this fashion
by way of experiment. [69]

171

It certainly looks as though the stage is being set for the appearance of the Dictator.

BIG BROTHER IS WATCHING

Further technological developments indicate that total surveillance by a dictator is a very real possibility. In a book entitled *Fiber Optics: The Eye of the Antichrist*, communications scientists Dr. Emil Gaverluk and Dr. Patrick Fisher discuss the implications of the fiber optics which are beginning to be widely used to transmit telephone and television sound and video signals. The fiber optics are described, in laymen's terms, as a "two-way light and sound pipe" capable of not only bringing a signal into a home but of actually *monitoring* a room through a pinhead-sized fish-eye lens on the cable end.

The question in the future, as someone put it with wry humor, will not be "Are you watching your TV?" but "Is your *TV watching you?*"—especially since the fiber optics have the capacity to transmit even when a set is off![70] Certainly, with the rapid technological development being seen today, the prospect of a George Orwell *1984* scenario, in which it is impossible to escape the eye of Big Brother, is very much a reality.

When to these facts is added the growing global problems that demand some strong solution, the feasibility of a world dictator grows.

WE NEED A LEADER

The Club of Rome in 1976 issued another of its reports entitled *RIO—Reshaping the International Order* in which a group of 21 international specialists presented, in detail, the desperate need for a new "one world" approach to government—on a "functional basis."

Hal Lindsey in *The Late Great Planet Earth* quotes the eminent historian Arnold Toynbee as saying on a late 1960s radio broadcast, "By forcing on mankind more and more lethal weapons, and at the same time making the world more and more interdependent economically, technology has brought mankind to such a degree of distress that we are ripe for the deifying of any new Caesar who might succeed in giving the world unity and peace." [71]

What would Toynbee say almost two decades later?

Henry Spaak, at the time Secretary General of NATO, said, "We do not want another committee; we have too many already. What we want is a man of sufficient stature to hold the allegiance of all people and to lift us out of the economic morass into which we are sinking. Send us such a man and *be he god or devil, we will receive him"* (italics mine).[72]

Such a Satan-energized, diabolically capable person will indeed appear—just as the prophets foretold.

WHAT ABOUT THE TEMPLE?

Consider one other factor. The Antichrist will demand to be worshipped as God in a restored Jewish Temple. Are there any moves afoot today to rebuild such a place of worship?

There certainly has been much speculation and discussion about a temple on the site currently occupied by the Moslem Dome of the Rock. In addition, serious references to the rebuilding of the Jewish Temple have appeared in respected journals like *Time*, *Christianity Today*, *The Jewish Press*, *Jerusalem Post* and others.

When Israel recaptured the Old City of Jerusalem with its remains of the Temple in 1967, the aged Jewish historian Israel Eldad was quoted in *Time* as saying, "We are at the stage which David was when he liberated Jerusalem. From that time until the construction of the Temple by Solomon only one generation passed. So will it be with us."

Asked about the Moslem shrine, the Dome of the Rock, now on the site, Eldad replied, "It is of course an open question. Who knows? Perhaps there will be an earthquake."[73]

It is a fact that several attempts in Israel to get a popular people's movement going to rebuild the Temple have been discouraged by the Israeli government, probably for political reasons in view of the Muslim regard for the Dome of the Rock, considered to be Islam's second most sacred site.

The question is a mystifying one. We know there will be a temple—and we know that there is a good deal of interest in and talk about its reconstruction (including some reports since proven inaccurate that stones for it had been cut and shipped from Indiana to Jerusalem). But how and when this temple will be constructed we don't know.

Charles R. Taylor of *Today in Bible Prophecy* writes that

> ...a special school has been established to train young Israelis of the tribe of Levi in the ancient rites of sacrifice. Called "Yeshiva Avodas Hakodesh," the school was founded by Rabbi Hirsh Ha-Cohen. It was dedicated at the time of the Feast of Dedication (Chanuka) in December, 1970.
>
> The very religious Jews called "hasidim" wear "payos" (long strands of hair on the sides of their faces) and are very strict in their religious observances. Only students who can trace their ancestry to Aaron, the first

Kohain, are admitted to Yeshiva Avodas Hakodesh.

There they learn the laws of ancient animal sacrifice and how to perform the practices which existed in the ancient Holy Temple.

The Kohanim intend to be ready as soon as the temple can be built. They believe that the repeated victories of this generation, and especially the conquest of Jerusalem, indicate that the Messiah is about to appear. [74]

Whether we are on the verge of seeing the Temple reconstructed, or whether the Great Synagogue, which has recently been built in Jerusalem, could be the Tribulation Temple, as some believe, is a point on which it is not wise to be too dogmatic.

The very fact, however, that the Temple reconstruction is once again a point of serious discussion is another indication that the time of the Antichrist's rule must be drawing near.

I don't want, nor expect, to be around when he comes on the scene.

For Further Reading:

Satan in the Sanctuary by T. McCall and Z. Levitt

The Mark is Ready—Are You? by R. Steele

The Cashless Society by Wally Wood Jr.

9

Meanwhile—On the Religious Scene

During my middle childhood, an elderly uncle
used to occasionally visit us for several days at a
time. Invariably on such occasions the
conversation would turn to certain aspects of
prophecy, since my uncle, whom I highly
respected and slightly feared, was an avid
student of future events. I can vividly recall my
father and uncle discussing prophetic topics,
often far into the night. I would usually fall
asleep straining my ears from my bedroom to
follow their conversation.

One topic in particular often recurred and
tended to cause me, as a young child, a good
deal of concern. My uncle had accepted, and
thereafter strongly propounded, an interpretation of Revelation chapters 17 and 18 which has
been held by some biblical students for many
years. That view is that the "harlot" of
Revelation is a particular church—which will be
left nameless. Uncle Fred would wax eloquent
"proving" how this was so, and describing the

dangers of it all! Consequently, I used to really keep my distance from all members and aspects of that church because, even though I wasn't absolutely certain uncle was right, I wanted to be *sure* I was safe! I have since come to believe very strongly that my uncle—and the school of interpretation to which he subscribed—was only *partially* right.

IT IS A CHURCH

I am convinced that the "harlot" of Revelation is *indeed* a church—in fact, a powerful global religious system—but I am also quite certain it is *not* the particular church my uncle believed it to be...with all due respect to his memory. I believe the "harlot church" definitely will contain elements of *that* church and many, many others—but that it will not be just any *one* church.

Now—if all of this talk of a church being a "harlot," and of a powerful global religion is confusing to you, please "hang tough" as we attempt to explain.

LET'S DEFINE THE TERMS

Let's start with some definitions.

A harlot is a woman who has prostituted her God-given sexuality in order to sell her body's sexual functions to any number of "lovers"—in direct contrast to a wife who becomes one with her husband in a faithful, pure union.

The man/woman relationship is frequently found in Scripture as a symbol of spiritual relationships. For example, the symbol used in Scripture to describe the Church (the body of born-again believers from around the world through the ages) is that of a Bride. In Ephesians 5, and in Revelation 19, the Lord Jesus Christ is depicted as the Bridegroom— the One to whom the true Church will be married. We who are believers are the Bride of Christ whose union has not yet been consummated. In the Old Testament, Israel was said by God to have been married to Him, with sin and straying being described as "adultery."

Spiritual departure from God is frequently symbolized in Scripture by the use of terms like "adultery," "whoredom," "harlotry." A woman used symbolically in Scripture signifies religion. A good woman, like a "bride" or "wife," means good religion—the true Church. A bad woman, like a "harlot," means an evil religious sytem that deceives the souls of humanity.

So when the prophet John used the term "harlot" in describing the vision he had received, he was unquestionably writing about a religious sytem which had *prostituted* its very existence to that which is totally contradictory to the true purpose of the Church.

Look at what John was inspired by God to write in Revelation 17. Remember as you do that the "harlot" represents a false church, and the strange beast upon which she rides represents a confederacy of nations. Read the prophecy carefully and then consider its explanation:

> And there came one of the seven angels which had the seven vials, and talked with me, saying unto me, Come higher; I will shew unto thee the judgment of the great whore that sitteth upon many waters.
>
> With whom the kings of the earth have committed fornication, and the inhabitants of the earth have been made drunk with the wine of her fornication.
>
> So he carried me away in the spirit into the wilderness: and I saw a woman sit upon a scarlet coloured beast, full of names of blasphemy, having seven heads and ten horns.
>
> And the woman was arrayed in purple and scarlet colour, and decked with gold and precious stones and pearls, having a golden cup in her hand full of abominations and filthiness of her fornication:
>
> And upon her forehead was a name

written, MYSTERY, BABYLON THE GREAT, THE MOTHER OF HARLOTS AND ABOMINATIONS OF THE EARTH.

And I saw the woman drunken with the blood of the saints, and with the blood of the martyrs of Jesus: and when I saw her, I wondered with great admiration.

And the angel said unto me, Wherefore didst thou marvel? I will tell thee the mystery of the woman, and of the beast that carrieth her, which hath the seven heads and ten horns.

The beast that thou sawest was, and is not; and shall ascend out of the bottomless pit, and go into perdition: and they that dwell on the earth shall wonder, whose names were not written in the book of life from the foundation of the world, when they behold the beast that was, and is not, and yet is.

And here is the mind which hath wisdom. The seven heads are seven mountains, on which the woman sitteth.

And there are seven kings: five are fallen, and one is, and the other is not yet come; and when he cometh, he must continue a short space.

And the beast that was, and is not, even he is the eighth, and is of the seven, and goeth into perdition.

And the ten horns which thou sawest are ten kings, which have received no kingdom as yet; but receive power as kings one hour with the beast.

These have one mind, and shall give their power and strength unto the beast.

These shall make war with the Lamb, and the Lamb shall overcome them: for he is Lord of lords, and King of kings: and they that are with him are called, and chosen, and faithful.

And he saith unto me, The waters which thou sawest, where the whore sitteth, are peoples, and multitudes, and nations, and tongues.

And the ten horns which thou sawest upon the beast, these shall hate the whore, and shall make her desolate and naked, and shall eat her flesh, and burn her with fire.

For God hath put in their hearts to fulfil his will, and to agree, and give their kingdom unto the beast, until the words of God shall be fulfilled.

And the woman which thou sawest is that great city, which reigneth over the kings of the earth.

Revelation 17:1-18

WHAT DOES IT MEAN?

The two main figures in this prophecy are as

fascinating as they are repulsive and weird.

The "harlot" is described as lavishly decked in jewels and gorgeous garments, holding a rich gold cup—attractive on the outside, but full of putrefaction inside. Written across her forehead is the name "Babylon the Great, Mother of Harlots and the Abomination of the Earth." Most disgusting of all is the fact that she is drunk—but not with wine. She is drunk with the blood of saints and martyrs.

This brazen woman sits upon a seven-headed beast—standing near a great body of water—with the seventh head having ten horns. The Beast turns upon the "harlot," strips her and devours her, finally burning her remains with fire.

Now, as I have suggested, this "harlot" is obviously the substitute for the Bride of Christ, the true Church. She will spiritually seduce not only kings (that is, she will not only wield control over the leaders of nations) but also mankind in common. This is clearly indicated by the explanation that the waters by which the "harlot" sits are peoples, nations, races (17:15). All mankind, apart from the saints, is included.

SUCH A PERVERSE SYSTEM

But what kind of religion could possibly hold such sway and gain such control over Moslems,

Hindus, Christians (the *nominal* kind only since the Church will have been raptured by this time), Buddhists, atheists and so on?

Quite apparently, no *one* religion like Protestantism, or Islam, or Catholicism could get *all* the other religions to join it, though many such attempts have been and are being made. Unquestionably, whatever religion it is, it will have to have a strong appeal—far stronger than the pull of watered-down liberal Christianity today.

What sort of religion could this be?

The solution to the mystery is found in the name on the "harlot's" forehead: "Babylon the Great." The "harlot" religious system is thus associated with Babylon—a city which was more than just a city. It was an entity which, as far as the world of its day was concerned, embodied in itself *a world church, a world empire*, and *a world ruler* whom all nations were compelled to worship as supreme. Thus, depraved religion, enforced by government decree and a sinful, lustful lifestyle, comes to mind when Babylon is mentioned.

Proper biblical interpretation, which demands that the first use of a term in Scripture be followed in every successive use, soon confirms that we are close to solving the mystery of what religion the "harlot" could possibly represent.

Babylon was born when the first "world ruler," Nimrod (whose name meant "we will revolt''), built Babylon on the Plains of Shinar in the process of constructing his kingdom (Genesis 10:8-10). The first united religious act undertaken by mankind was the construction of a tower whose top would reach into the heavens (Genesis 11:4). This was the famed Tower of Babel.

There has been much misunderstanding about this tower. Those first Babylonians were *not* attempting to build a tower which could actually reach the heavens. They weren't that stupid. Rather, they were building an astrological tower—a ziggurat—which could be used to study the stars, chart their courses, cast horoscopes and make predictions. *Halley's Bible Handbook* declares that idolatrous worship was the whole purpose for the construction of the ziggurats.[75]

The prophet Isaiah, in chapter 47:12,13, indicates that Babylon "labored with sorceries and astrology from her youth"—from the very beginnings of her history. Isaiah also prophesied that Babylon could not be delivered by her prognosticators—indicating that these practices were deeply engrained in Babylon's life.

It is a fact that astrology, sorcery, clairvoyance, conjuring and magic had their origins in the writings of the Chaldeans, who divided the heavens into the twelve sections of the Zodiac and claimed that the stars control the destiny of mankind.

185

This religion, which obviously had its roots in the effort to build the tower of Babel, reached its pinnacle in the Babylonian Empire. History reveals that each of the Babylonian rulers built giant ziggurats for the use of their astrologers and Chaldeans.

DANIEL ADDS SOME DETAILS

The book of Daniel, which we considered in chapter six, lists the magicians, astrologers (conjurers), sorcerers and Chaldeans whom Nebuchadnezzar summoned to reveal his dream and its interpretation. These religious practitioners dealt in black magic, contact with demon spirits, materialization, witchcraft and astrology. According to Hal Lindsey in *There's a New World Coming*, the Chaldeans were a special priestly caste who could trace their family history back to the very originators of the art of astrology.

The name Babylon, then, is synonymous with a false religious system begun in Babylon that includes the occultic practices—such as black magic, seances, demon contact, miracles, witchcraft, sorcery and astrology.

The "harlot" represents this religion. Her dazzling external appearance suggests the appeal the system has to the sensual nature. The gold cup full of putridness symbolizes the corruption of her teachings, while her intoxication with the blood of believers indicates her method of dealing with those who oppose her.

And, for the first part of John's prophecy, the "harlot" rides or controls the Beast. In other words, the religious sytem rules the nations. John is saying that an occultic amalgamation of the world's religions—the revived Babylonian religion—will control the final world power.

A look at Revelation 17:9 and 10 confirms this. Here's what the prophet says:

> And here is the mind which hath wisdom. The seven heads are seven mountains, on which the woman sitteth.
> And there are seven kings: five are fallen, and one is, and the other is not yet come; and when he cometh, he must continue a short space.

This tells us that the seven heads of the beast represent *two* things: seven mountains and seven kingdoms. The seven mountains undoubtedly refer to Rome—a city known around the world to be built upon seven hills.

The city of Rome in John's time was indeed controlled by the Babylonian religious sytem. It was the center of pagan worship and was even called "Babylon" in Scripture.

But the seven heads are also seven kingdoms...and there's more information given about these. Note Revelation 17:10 and 12:

And there are seven kings: five are
fallen, and one is, and the other is not
yet come; and when he cometh, he must
continue a short space.

And the ten horns which thou sawest
are ten kings, which have received no
kingdom as yet; but receive power as
kings one hour with the beast.

Five of the seven kingdoms had fallen, one
was in existence at the time John wrote and one
was yet to come—the seventh. The seventh is to
be different from the rest—having ten horns.

THE SEVEN KINGDOMS

Now what does history reveal? Have there
been seven kingdoms controlled by the religion
of Babylon? Indeed, there have been six so far.

THE FIVE THAT "ARE FALLEN." The first
of these was *Assyria*, with its capital of Nineveh
given over to the occult as Nahum 3:4 clearly
shows.

Next was *Egypt*, which has left us evidence of
her preoccupation with the occult in those
fabulously costly pyramids—all built according
to astrological specification. The sphinx is
supposedly the key to the twelve sections of the
Zodiac.

Then there was the *Babylonian* empire, in

188

which Daniel lived and served God. The Babylonian religious sytem obviously reached its zenith during this empire.

Medo-Persia conquered Babylon but was in turn "enslaved by the Babylonian religion."

The fifth of the five which had fallen by John's time was *Greece*—in which occultic religion also held sway, as history abundantly reveals.

These empires all had in common an underlying belief in astrology, which bound together witchcraft, sorcery and magic. The practitioners of these arts usually enjoyed great stature and power—with kings seldom making any move without first consulting advisors steeped in Babylon's ancient occultic art.[76]

THE ONE "THAT IS." John referred to a kingdom that "is"—which also came under the sway of the occultic beliefs that have their origin on the plains of Shinar at the Tower of Babel. There can be no doubt that this was the mighty empire of *Rome*, whose dependence upon her augurs, sorcerers and astrologers has been immortalized in Shakespeare's Roman plays such as *Julius Caesar*.

THE ONE THAT IS "YET TO COME." This leaves only the seventh kingdom, the one described as "the other is not yet come; and when it comes it must continue a short while."

Recalling our discussion of Daniel's prophecy about the ten-nation confederacy arising out of the old Roman Empire, and comparing it with the ten horns of John's symbolic beast, it is obvious that this kingdom "yet to come," to be influenced by the ancient religion of Babylon, seems to be the revived Roman Empire—the *European Common Market*.

Now, having provided this panorama of world powers seduced by the "harlot," the prophet narrows his focus to the final world power—"the beast that was, and is not and will be"—and says that this king will be destroyed (17:11).

John says "even he is the eighth." His destruction fits the picture we have had sketched elsewhere, when we recall (as was discussed in chapter eight) that the Antichrist, who takes charge of the revived Roman Empire, later sets *himself* up as God.

This satanic culmination of the adulterous religious activity of a sinful, rebellious mankind is in effect the eighth and final form of this diabolical, counterfeit system. But in deifying himself, the Antichrist will destroy the Harlot. Though the revived Roman Empire is initially controlled by the religious system (and the Antichrist apparently goes along with it), the two are strange bedfellows. Each is trying to use the other.

Thus, at the midpoint of the seven-year treaty the Antichrist decides he no longer needs the false church. He and the false prophet have become wonder workers themselves—energized by Satan. Thus, he proclaims himself to be god—and the harlot is destroyed by him. How ironic!

COULD IT HAPPEN?

Is there anything on the world religious scene today that would cause us to believe that these events could occur in the near future? I believe there is.

There are at least three trends in the world today which appear to be foreshadowings of the "harlot's" appearance.

The *first* is the continuing drive for a one-world church—regardless of doctrine or even religion. If you're not "into" this sort of thing you may not be aware of the fact that a World Council of Churches exists and has as its goal the unification of all religions—Protestant, Catholic, Buddhist, Jewish—and so on.

The World Council of Churches traces its roots back to the Universal Christian Council on Life and Work, held in Stockholm, Sweden, in 1925. Joint conferences between this Council and the older International Missionary Council resulted in the formation, in Amsterdam, of the World Council of Churches in 1948.

The WCC meets every seven years in a General Assembly of delegates appointed by member churches or religious organizations. A 150-member Central Committee meets every six months, but the real power resides in the Secretariat in Geneva.

As Dr. J. De Forest Murch says in *The Coming World Church*, the WCC

> is composed of a wide assortment of churches which have great differences in theological doctrine, church organization and worship. They represent many nationalities, political viewpoints and sociological backgrounds. They are unitarians and trinitarians.... There are dozens of different rites and liturgies of communion and worship. There are Soviet Russian Communists, other Communists, Socialists, Democrats and Republicans. [77]

The May 10, 1970, *Los Angeles Times* reported:

> A World Conference of Religions for Peace will be held at Kyoto, Japan, October 16 to 22, according to Dr. Maurice E. Eisendrath.
> It will be attended by representatives of the world's greatest faiths: Judeo-Christian, Buddhist, Hindu, Shintoist and others, said Dr. Eisendrath, president of the Union of American

Hebrew Congregations.... It will be the first attempt by the powerful leaders of the great faiths to find a common ground of belief on a matter central to most religions—that of PEACE for our time.

The conference, the first of its kind, also will send its message for peace, on behalf of most of the world's 3.5 billion people, to global political leaders, in a way that can scarcely be ignored....

Among the Christians invited, he added, were John Cardinal Wright of Vatican City, Dr. Eugene Carson Blake, general secretary of the World Council of Churches, and Dr. Michael Ramsey, Archbishop of Canterbury.

"Hardly a religion in the Orient or in the West will not be represented," said Dr. Eisendrath. "The far-reaching geographic representation will include leaders from behind the Iron Curtain, from Africa, and virtually every other corner of the world. It will be unique. *Its goal will be to mobilize the religious constituency of the world, and to apply respective teachings of peace to the achievement of PEACE....*" [78]

On June 11, 1970, *Christian Beacon* reported:

"Theologians Take Steps in Dialogue

With Men of Other Faiths" is the
heading to a story reported from Zurich,
Switzerland, by Ecumenical Press
Service, June 2, 1970. The World
Council of Churches is the main
organization working for dialogue with
pagan faiths. The *EPS* story describes
the latest efforts for dialogue:

Christians must place their faith in
Christ in a positive relationship to the
faiths of other men if conversations
between each other should *neither*
betray the commitment of the Christian
nor exploit the confidence of men of
other faiths, 23 Christian theologians
said here recently. They were attending
a consultation on "Christians in
dialogue with men of other faiths"
which was a follow-up to the recent
World Council-sponsored conference
between Hindus, Buddhists, Christians
and Muslims in Ajaltoun, Lebanon.

The theologians here noted that the
demand for conversations has focused
attention on certain questions about the
mission of the Church that must be
reconsidered....

"Dialogue" also raises new questions
for Christians living in multi-religious
communities such as taking part in the
struggle of all people for justice and
PEACE. [79]

The WCC has been the center of a great deal of controversy recently over its policy of granting funds to militant rebel groups—a total of $2.6 million since 1969, according to a March 1979 report in *Eternity* magazine. One of the WCC funded groups—the Patriotic Front of Zimbabwe—has been accused of the 1978 murder of 40 Rhodesian missionaries. [80] Such a policy by a church body is quite apparently a prostitution of the biblical function of the Church.

Nevertheless, the grants continue. The drive for a world church was reemphasized at the WCC-related European Conference of Churches, October 1979, when Dr. Lukas Vischu, a Swiss Reform clergyman, and the Eastern Orthodox Ecumenical patriarch Dimitrios I, united in urging the Roman Catholic church to join forces with the World Council of Churches. [81]

While the goal of a single global church has undoubtedly been in the minds of churchmen for many years, the concrete efforts to achieve it are only of recent vintage. Now the amazing spread of the philosophy of secular humanism, defined in the *Humanist Manifestos I* and *II*, published in 1933 and 1973, has given this drive a powerful global push, especially in the West.

Certainly an ecumenized liberal church of externals, without real spiritual life, could easily accept all religions into one super-church in the climate which now exists.

THAT OLD BLACK MAGIC

A *second* trend is the turn to the *supernatural*—including the occult—on the part of North Americans, accompanied by a great revival of spiritism all over the world. At a conference in Arrowhead Springs, California, in late 1979, I heard Dr. Charles Malik, former President of the United Nations, cite the revival of paganism and spiritism as one of the most disturbing trends of our day.

Even in "sophisticated" America interest in witchcraft, the occult, the horoscope and numerous related supernatural topics has mushroomed.

Many magazines, like *McCalls, Esquire* and *Time*, ran feature articles at the beginning of the 1970s on what then was termed "the occult explosion." Movies, books, magazines and encyclopedias of the supernatural abound. Entire bookstores devoted to the occult are not uncommon. Universities regularly offer courses on witchcraft and magic—usually the so-called "white" variety. Myriads of mystical Eastern religions, bizarre and often demonic, have invaded North America—discovering in most cases an amazing responsiveness.

Some time ago, I visited a neighbor who was hospitalized in a nearby city. As we sat and chatted I was amazed to see, out on the lawn of the hospital, a young woman engaged in a series of physical gyrations that suggested to my mind a form of bizarre worship. I later discovered that her antics were, indeed, acts of worship to an Eastern deity! And this in public—in a "Bible-belt" section of conservative Canada!

THE "TURNED ON" CROWD

Then there's the *drug epidemic*, which scarcely needs to be documented. The reason for its being related to the emergence of a one-world counterfeit church does need to be spelled out, however.

In Revelation 9:21, a group of people whom the prophet foresees as experiencing the judgments of God are described as, in spite of that judgment, "repenting not of their murders, nor of their sorceries, nor of their fornication, nor of their thefts." The nationally-known Canadian evangelist, Barry Moore, in a message on the source of the drug problem, points out that the world translated "sorceries" in the above portion is significant. It comes from the Greek word *pharmakeia* which is the word from which we get our English word "pharmacy"—or drug store. It means a drug-related kind of occult worship or black magic. [82]

And Revelation 18—referring to the false "harlot's" religious system—charges that "all the nations were deceived by your *sorcery*" —

using the same word, *pharmakeia*.

There can be little question that Satan uses hallucinatory drugs to take people to a deeper level of satanic influence and control. An individual for whom I, along with others, had the awesome privilege of obtaining deliverance from deep entanglement in witchcraft and demonic control confirms that this is so—from personal experience and observation.

So when these three trends are observed to be having a strong impact on the world, it is apparent that the prophecies concerning "mystery Babylon" must be in the early stages of their fulfillment.

An additional comment must be made here concerning the belief (held by some observers of the religious scene) that certain aspects of the charismatic movement could be a unifying factor in terms of the final phony super-church.

It *is* a fact that a wide variety of groups, ranging all the way from bona fide Pentecostals, through cults like "The Way," to pagan, eastern and Satanic religions, practice speaking in unknown tongues.

It is also a fact that the charismatic experience in some Christian circles tends to make people ready and willing to accept fellow charismatics *regardless* of their stand on biblical or doctrinal matters.

While I do recognize that there is a true and valid charisma, such attitudes as described above provide a basis for the view that a strong *counterfeit* charismatic movement *could* be a powerful added force in creating the "harlot" church. If indeed a counterfeit charismatic element does play a future role, certainly what is occurring in the world today has to be viewed (at the very least) as creating the climate for such a pressure for religious union.

BABYLON RISES AGAIN?

One other current event is of interest. The actual city of Babylon is being rebuilt by the Iraq government, which in 1971 announced plans to complete the restoration of the ancient city by 1982, complete with the hanging gardens, once considered among the seven wonders of the world. The project is costing multiplied millions—much of it being contributed by oil-rich Arab individuals.

And a Religious News Service item out of Tokyo early in 1980 indicates:

> "Reconstruction" of the biblical Tower of Babel is under consideration by a team of academics from Japan's Kyoto University.
>
> A spokesman for the team said that the Iraqi government had requested help from Japan to create a "museum city" out of the ancient city of Babylon as a tourist center on the Euphrates

River about 55 miles south of Baghdad.

The long-considered project, the spokesman said, calls for partial restoration of Babylon with rebuilding of the Tower of Babel....

The Kyoto University team, at Iraq's request, also proposes to rebuild the great Ishtar Gate of Babylon, which opened on a street that led to the temple of Marduk.

In addition, the team will make a detailed proposal later in the year for construction of a museum, a research center, and a modern traffic system to receive tourists in Babylon. [83]

Some prophetic students believe that a rebuilt Babylon could become the headquarters for the harlot church—pointing to the prophecy of Zechariah 5:5-11 as proof. It is not my intention to attempt to give here the reasoning behind this view—although it could have great merit. The point is that it seems significant, however one views it, that at *this* juncture in time, the city where it all got started so far as the false harlot religion is concerned, is being rebuilt.

It couldn't have happened even a few years ago. It wasn't all that long ago that the Arab nations couldn't even have rebuilt Nebuchadnezzar's *footstool*, let alone his *city*, which was once one of the mightiest metropolises in all the earth!

The pieces of the puzzle continue to come together!

For Further Reading:
  There's a New World Coming, pp. 240-249 by Hal Lindsey
  Hindus, Hippies, Rock 'n Roll by Bob Larson
  Babylon Reborn by Bob Larson
  The Late Great Planet Earth by Hal Lindsey

10

Planet Earth is Running Out

I heard the other day about a fellow who was a cigarette smoker. In his reading of newspaper reports and magazine articles, he came across many indications of the dangers of smoking and the way it is frequently related to lung cancer. As he continued to read these disturbing reports he became more and more concerned. Finally one day he said to a friend, "You know—I've been reading so much about smoking and cancer that I'm going to have to give up reading!"

Maybe we can identify with him.

It often seems these days that it would be nice to simply "give up reading" all of the disturbing reports about the serious conditions in our world that just keep coming every time we open a newspaper or turn on a radio or TV set. But, of course, ignoring our situation when we *can* do something would make as much sense as the smoker giving up his reading.

Instead, let's take a good hard look at the

many indications there are that our planet is "running out"—of resources, room, time and options in so many areas. And let's check to see whether the factors we'll consider have been related by the prophetic scriptures to the return of Christ. Then, let's arrange our lives and priorities in the light of this data.

A PROPHETIC PICTURE

The time was two days before the Lord Jesus Christ went to the cross. The setting was just outside the Temple. The disciples of Jesus were commenting upon the beauty of the Temple with its fine stonework and various ornamentations. Suddenly Jesus said, "Do you see all these things? Truly I say to you—there shall not be left one stone upon another that shall not be thrown down" (Matthew 24:2).

The disciples were astounded and later came to Jesus, privately, to ask Him three questions for clarification. They inquired:

1. "When shall these things be?"

2. "What shall be the sign of your coming?", and

3. "[What shall be the sign] of the end of the world?" (Matthew 24:3).

Jesus gave them this reply, as recorded in both Matthew 24 and Luke 21. The account from Luke follows.

And he said, take heed that ye be not deceived: for many shall come in my name, saying, I am Christ; and the time draweth near: go ye not therefore after them.

But when ye shall hear of wars and commotions, be not terrified: for these things must first come to pass; but the end is not by and by.

Then said he unto them, Nation shall rise against nation, and kingdom against kingdom:

And great earthquakes shall be in divers places, and famines, and pestilences; and fearful sights and great signs shall there be from heaven.

But before all these, they shall lay their hands on you, and persecute you, delivering you up to the synagogues, and into prison, being brought before kings and rulers for my name's sake.

And it shall turn to you for a testimony.

Settle it therefore in your hearts, not to meditate before what ye shall answer:

For I will give you a mouth and wisdom, which all your adversaries shall not be able to gainsay nor resist.

And ye shall be betrayed both by parents, and brethren, and kinsfolks, and friends; and some of you shall they cause to be put to death.

And ye shall be hated of all men for my name's sake.

But there shall not an hair of your head perish.

In your patience possess ye your souls.

And when ye shall see Jerusalem compassed with armies, then know that the desolation thereof is nigh.

Then let them which are in Judaea flee to the mountains; and let them which are in the midst of it depart out; and let not them that are in the countries enter thereinto.

For these be the days of vengeance, that all things which are written may be fulfilled.

But woe unto them that are with child, and to them that give suck, in those days! for there shall be great distress in the land, and wrath upon this people.

And they shall fall by the edge of the sword, and shall be led away captive unto all nations: and Jerusalem shall be trodden down of the Gentiles, until the times of the Gentiles be fulfilled.

And there shall be signs in the sun, and in the moon, and in the stars; and upon the earth distress of nations, with perplexity: the sea and the waves roaring;

Men's hearts failing them for fear,

and for looking after those things which are coming on the earth: for the powers of heaven shall be shaken.

And then shall they see the Son of man coming in a cloud with power and great glory.

And when these things begin to come to pass, then look up, and lift up your heads; for your redemption draweth nigh.

Then Jesus related the parable of the fig tree (which we have already considered in chapter five) and stated that the generation which saw the events He had just described (the "putting forth of leaves" by the "fig tree" nation of Israel) would also see the fulfillment of *all*.

HOW SHOULD WE UNDERSTAND THIS?

Now before we actually look at what's happening in our world today we need to lay a few basic ground rules. Please bear with me while we become rather technical for a few paragraphs. It's important that we do so in order to avoid going off "half-cocked" in our conclusions.

There are three major methods of interpreting this prophecy of Jesus which we are considering:

One view says it was all fulfilled in the past

and applies only to what has already occurred. The problem with such a view is to explain how Jesus could have already returned—at the time of the destruction of Jerusalem!

A second view holds that the prophecy applies to this entire "church age" in which we now live, and especially the closing days of it. Proponents of the view hold that the Church thus experiences the Tribulation.

A third view, and the one held by this author, is that *the prophecy has exclusive reference to the Jewish nation and Jewish believers.* It also has a double reference—part of it having had its fulfillment when the Romans under Titus destroyed the Temple and Jerusalem, with the remainder yet to be fulfilled in the final period of God's dealing with the entire earth in relation to, and through, the Jewish nation.

Obviously, the actual signs of His appearing which Jesus prophesied had in many instances a prior fulfillment at Jerusalem's fall. But while they will be finally *literally* fulfilled in the last seven years prior to the establishment of Christ's kingdom upon earth, they will not burst *suddenly* upon the world. They will rather be preceded by a building toward their appearance. Just as a birth is preceded by birth pangs which increase in intensity and frequency, so these actual signs—the literal ones to occur right before the appearing of Christ—will be immediately preceded by similar signs or the *beginning* of the *same* signs

208

throughout the earth.

And, if the imminent return of Christ with His saints is indicated by the appearance of these indicators, how much nearer must be the snatching away of the Church which precedes the return by seven years?

(As a reminder, the sequence of events—including the two-part Rapture/Return aspect of Christ's second coming—is clearly spelled out in chapter three, if you want to do a quick review.)

So, to summarize these preliminary comments, the *actual* events prophesied by Jesus in Matthew 24 and Luke 21 will occur *between* the Rapture and the Return. The *indicators* we will consider now are *similar* events obviously building up to those actual fulfillments.

TEN IMPORTANT INDICATORS

A synopsis of the two accounts of Jesus' prophecy provides us with the following ten great indicators of His return:

One: Wars, and as a part of that sign, rumors of wars, commotions, nation rising against nation and kingdom against kingdom.

Two: Great earthquakes in various places.

Three: Famines.

Four: Pestilences.

Five: Unusual, frightening *signs in the heavens*, including fearful sights, great signs from the heavens, signs in the sun, moon and stars, with the powers of heaven being shaken.

Six: Jerusalem restored to Jewish control AFTER a worldwide dispersion and return to Israel by the Jews.

Seven: Distress of nations, *with perplexity.*

Eight: Men's hearts failing them for *fear* of what is coming on the earth.

Nine: False Christs.

Ten: A world-wide proclamation of the Gospel.

That's the list Jesus gave His disciples.

WHAT'S THE CURRENT SCENE?

As we set out to see what's happening in our world today in relationship to these indicators, I frankly confess a major problem. There is so much material about each of these that a whole chapter, or even an entire book, could be written on each one. My problem is to somehow adequately condense these mountains of data into the space available and still do justice to it all.

1. WARS. Throughout all of human history there have always been wars. Tragically, however, the tempo and severity of war is now rapidly increasing. In the twentieth century alone we have had 130 armed conflicts. There have been six ''minor'' costly wars: the

Russo-Japanese War (1904-05); the Balkan Wars (1912-13); the Spanish Civil War (1937-39); the Colombian Civil War (1948-53); the Korean War (1950-53); and the Vietnam War (1963-73). In these wars at least 2,000,000 soldiers and another 750,000 civilians died.

There have also been the two major World Wars in 1914-18 and 1939-45, in which 10 million (WW I) and 51 million (WW II) perished. [84]

Then there is presently occurring what Alexander Solzhenitsyn and many others term "World War III," which has gone on continuously since 1945. Former U.S. President Nixon in a book published in April 1980, claims "the West is losing this Third World War." [85]

The *Chicago Tribune*, in January 1980, published a news map which showed that at that moment 23 separate armed conflagrations were raging—involving some eight million soldiers and para-military personnel with casualties estimated at five million killed or wounded. [86]

Using Webster's definition of war as "open, armed conflict between countries, military operations as a department of activity or any active hostility or contention, conflict, strife," the view that there has been a state of war for years is, without question, true. Since 1945 some two dozen countries with an area of more than four and one-half million square miles and a total population of well over one billion have

211

been conquered by Communism.

So far as *rumors of war* are concerned, it's the rare issue of any major news magazine today, or of the past few years, that doesn't have at least one article on conflict, its frightful prospect, the arms race, or the economic battle.

Furthermore, by the end of the current decade 35 nations are expected to have nuclear capacity. Chemical and technological weaponry is feverishly being developed. The world becomes increasingly a gigantic armed camp. The thought, even to those of us who know only a *bit* about it, is terrifying!

It's not going to get any better either.

There are three more *major* conflagrations on earth's prophetic timetable at which we'll look in chapter twelve.

2. EARTHQUAKES. Again, earthquakes are not unique to our age. But as with wars, their frequency and severity is dramatically increasing.

Dr. John Wesley White, in his book *World War III*, quotes a prominent historian of seismology who after nearly a lifetime of study reckons that major earthquakes have increased from 137 in the fourteenth century to thousands in our present century. All around the world, major (over magnitude seven on the Richter Scale) killer quakes are taking hundreds of thousands of lives.[87] In an article entitled ''The Age of Disaster,'' a *Gemini News Service* writer says that experts warn that "we are in the age of earthquakes. The period up to the middle 1980s will be one of exceptional activity."

A *Time* cover feature in September 1975, "Forecast: Earthquake," contained a chilling scenario of San Francisco during the expected major San Andreas fault movement. [88] Since then (on April 18, 1980, the 74th Anniversary of the 1906 quake) the city of San Francisco staged a mock earthquake and disaster drill—in preparation for "The Big One." [89]

3. FAMINES. The tragic truth is that much of the world is on the verge of starvation, a fact hard to believe in affluent North America where dieting and exercising away excess pounds is a major industry. It is true nonetheless.

Paul Ehrlich, the renowned Stanford biologist, has written *The End of Affluence, The Population Bomb* and *How to be a Survivor*. He concludes that "it is shockingly apparent that the battle to feed man will end in a rout."

A major *Time* magazine Special Report in December of 1975 sketched a grim picture of "Poor vs. Rich: A New Global Conflict" in the struggle for survival and for enough food to live. [90]

Since then, *in spite of record high food production in the late 70s,* the World Food Council meeting in Ottawa in 1979 was told that "More go hungry than ever before." Newspaper headlines in early 1980 tell the frightening tale: "Famine Plagues Brazil," "Unchecked Food Shortages will Cause Disaster, UN says" and "Food Crises in East Africa." [91]

A March 12, 1980, Canadian Press release declares that the World Food Bank estimates that the problem of starvation could exceed all previous grim "dimensions."[92]

We've heard it so often that we're immune to the tragedy of it all—but it's a fact. Famine—on a global scale—is upon us *even in good times!* What if conditions become severe?

4. PESTILENCES. A related sign is that of pestilence. The following report entitled "Superbugs: A New Biblical Plague?" from the *Sunday Oregonian Parade*, September 30, 1979, indicates something of how serious this threat is:

Insects, once decimated by pesticides, have developed immunities enabling them to multiply at a fantastic pace, posing a threat to world crops. The battle erupts in Texas. After years of being kept under control, a generation of insects begins multiplying in fantastic numbers—suddenly unaffected by the chemical weapons that have kept them in check. Farmers get panicky, some spraying their fields as many as 50 times with powerful insecticides, but it has little effect.

After devouring much of the Texas cotton crop, the insects march into northern Mexico, gobbling a million more acres of cotton, wiping out an entire industry, and leaving the land wasted and barren.

Newer and more exotic poisons are thrown at them but serve only to slow the insects down. After shaking off the new assault, the voracious hordes regroup and sweep into Louisiana, eating a quarter of that state's cotton crop. Temporarily sated, they head west to California, bringing terror to the lush Imperial Valley, America's vegetable bowl.

Here, the crawling, wriggling juggernaut begins chomping its way through some 5 billion pounds of lettuce—three quarters of the nation's crop. All seems lost until a last-ditch defense with another new poison thwarts the assault. America's salad bowls are safe this year, but the victory may be only temporary. Where will the monster bugs strike next?

This may sound like the scenario of a Hollywood horror movie, but the saga of the budworm (which is equally happy eating tobacco, cotton, lettuce and tomatoes—plus DDT, toxaphene,

215

methyl parathion and other powerful insecticides) is very real. Last winter's California lettuce crop was saved only after authorities agreed to the emergency use of a highly toxic and largely untested new pyrethroid chemical.

The budworm is just one of 364 so-called "superbugs" worldwide that have developed resistance to the witches' cauldron of poisons used to destroy them or keep them in check. They are the shock troops of a global insect army locked in constant combat with man, challenging us for our food and fiber supplies and bringing death, disease and discomfort to millions, particularly in Asia, Africa and Latin America.

Viewed in terms of war, it is the insects that are on the offensive. "They are beginning to tip the scales in their favor," warns Dr. Paul Schwartz, a U.S. Department of Agriculture (USDA) entomologist. "The potential for disaster is always present—in agriculture or in disease."

The United Nations Environment Program, in its recent State of the World report, noted with alarm the rapid gains made by insects, mites, ticks, rodents, weeds and fungi in becoming increasingly resistant to pesticides. This poses a grave threat to world health and food production.

Of the 364 superbugs, 223 are agricultural pests that attack crops in the fields or after the harvest. The remaining 141 spread disease to livestock or humans—flies, ticks, cockroaches, lice and mosquitoes.

In the last two years, the U.S. has been invaded by exploding populations of pests. Plagues of grasshoppers almost Biblical in size have blanketed and denuded millions of acres of crop and range lands in 14 states west of the Missouri River.

In Maine, millions—perhaps billions—of tent caterpillars have been defoliating trees and invading homes. Gypsy moths have stripped half a million acres of Pennsylvania forest and are spreading south into the Blue Ridge Mountains. Colorado is losing 2 million Ponderosa pines each year on the eastern slopes of the Rockies due to pine beetle infestation. Elsewhere, record numbers of borer, rootworms, bollworms, cutworms, webworms, hoppers, miners, loopers, beetles and weevils are decimating crops, making life miserable for farmers and homeowners, and causing millions of dollars in losses.

Overseas, the effects on food supplies

and public health are even more drastic as the insect hordes gather momentum. Locusts—bigger and more voracious cousins of the grasshopper—have swarmed across Africa and parts of Asia, eating everything from crops to wooden fence posts. Increasing resistance to insecticides is being shown by major pests that attack crops on which entire agricultural economies are based—rice in Japan, coconuts in tropical Africa, cattle in Australia, cereals everywhere.

The World Health Organization (WHO) has charted an alarming rise in malaria after seeing the disease dramatically reduced in recent years by effective new insecticides. But the mosquitoes have been highly successful in blunting these attacks by developing immunity. So far, 43 species that carry malaria—plus 41 species that transmit dengue, yellow fever and a host of dread tropical diseases—have developed resistance.

This country also faces a constant threat from mosquito-borne disease. Without expensive, continuing control programs, coastal areas of Florida and some Southern States would be uninhabitable. Dr. Donald Weidhaas, director of a USDA research laboratory in Gainsville, Fla., worries about the increasing resistance trend.

"We're lucky we can afford these expensive methods to combat the problem. The developing countries cannot," he says. "The potential is here for malaria and encephalitis; already we're seeing dengue and yellow fever turn up in Caribbean countries."

Changes in climate, different methods of agriculture and the banning of certain insecticides for environmental reasons are all contributing to the burgeoning insect populations. But resistance to chemicals—our first line of attack and defense—is the major and most worrisome reason. [93]

Killer bees and the dreaded fire ants from South America are another two of the more widely publicized of these superbugs. Their inexorable advance inspires terror as they march steadily northward up the North American continent. [94]

And in 1979, according to a Rome, Italy, United Press International release, "The Eighth Plague has Returned," astronomical numbers of locusts—described by Jean Roy, U.N. locust specialist, as "too many and too late to kill"—are devastating Africa and Arabia and threatening disaster. [95]

But perhaps the most serious pestilence of all

is the pestilence of the pollution of our atmosphere. The most recent threat is acid rain, that "scourge from the skies" which the June 1980 *Reader's Digest* calls "a deadly environmental threat that disregards international boundaries." [96]

Then there are the pestilences of *venereal disease*, which has become globally epidemic;* *bubonic plague*, or the "Black Death" as it was called, which is getting a grip once more in areas of Asia; and *cholera*, which is again rearing its head, and according to *Time* (June 21, 1971) took some 5,000 lives in one outbreak alone. [97]

Add *leprosy*, now affecting fifteen million of earth's people; *cancer*, the dreaded killer; and other factors, like *stress*, which is a major lifestyle problem throughout North America, and we're a plagued people. So—even technological, sophisticated twentieth-century man faces the serious challenge of pestilence, almost helplessly, it seems, as prophecy appears to indicate.

---

* The July 24, 1980, issue of **Time** carried an article on "Herpes: The New Sexual Leprosy," claiming that the "viruses of love" are infecting millions with disease and despair. [98]

5. UNUSUAL OCCURRENCES IN THE HEAVENS. An Air Canada *Enroute* magazine article I picked up on a May 1979 flight entitled "What's Happening to the Weather?" was introduced by this paragraph: "If you think we've been getting clobbered a lot harder and a lot more often recently, you are not imagining it. From all over Canada—indeed, from all over the world—the message is coming in: something weird is happening to the earth's weather and climate." [99]

Cliff Harris, a Montana climatologist and businessman, who operates his own private weather service, is a man with an exceptionally fine record of accuracy in both long- and short-term forecasts. In fact, syndicated columnist John Stromnes, in January 4, 1978, compared Harris to Immanuel Velikovsky—the Nobel Prize winning Russian scientist! Harris, in a forecast published in the November 16, 1978, issue of *The Whitefish* [*Montana*] *Pilot*, says that "the next decade may well become the most violent, weatherwise, in the past 4,000-plus years...since the chaotic days of Noah."

Disastrous storms, a mid-1980s 30-month U.S. drought, topsy-turvy world weather, falling mean global temperatures and cataclysmic winter in 1983-84 as a result of a sunspot and tornado cycle—are all part of Harris's predictions.

He doesn't claim to be error-free, but he has certainly been accurate to date, especially when his detailed 1978 forecasts and the weather of 1980 are compared! [100]

The prestigious Kiplinger Washington Letter of July 25, 1980, notes that, while the dozens of weather experts and forecasters to whom their editors had talked were not convinced that basic weather patterns are really changing, neither were they "looking down their noses at sunspot" and other theories anymore. [101]

With a killer heat wave and drought responsible for over 1,200 deaths in a half dozen U.S. southcentral states, record cold in Europe, unprecedented rains and floods in Canada and other areas, the summer of 1980 presented what could be a grim forerunner of what is still worse to come.

Then there is the phenomenon of the UFOs. Numerous books have been written on the subject, most seeking to prove the existence of these mysterious objects which in periodic waves of occurrences have invaded our heavens. In the late 1970s, a movie on the subject—"Close Encounters of the Third Kind"—became very popular.

One of the best books I've come across—and I've done a good deal of research on UFOs—is *Encounters with UFOs* by John Weldon. Weldon points out that, while accounts of UFOs are to be found even in ancient history, the number of recorded sightings for *all* time up to 1954 was around ten thousand. Since then there has been a dramatic increase of sightings into the *millions*! [102]

Subject of not only books and movies, but of a good deal of research by both government and private organizations like Project Bluebook, NICAP, APRO and others—UFOs have buzzed the White House (in 1952) and numerous defense sites. [103] They have been the subject also of an NBC TV Special on December 15, 1974, entitled "UFOs—Do You Believe?"

Weldon makes an extremely well-documented, reasoned and sane case for the view that UFOs are demonic and, as such, are definite indicators of the impending return of Christ. The subject is too deep to attempt to get into here—except to point out that these objects in the sky, coming as they appear to do in waves of sightings, certainly qualify as "signs in the heavens."

6. JERUSALEM RESTORED TO THE JEWS. This subject has already been considered at some length in chapter five. It is a fact of history that Jerusalem was finally and fully lost by the Jews in A.D. 70. The Jews were dispersed worldwide and—until June 6, 1967—the city of Jerusalem was controlled by non-Jewish, that is, Gentile, peoples. On that 1967 date, the ancient holy city once again fell into Jewish hands, and, in the opinion of most Bible

scholars, an era (the time of the Gentiles) came to a close.

7 and 8. DISTRESS OF NATIONS and FEAR. To avoid redundancy, let's combine the seventh and eighth indicators mentioned since they, perhaps more than any others, are very closely related.

One scarcely finds it necessary to document the fact that there is great distress among the nations today. The political leaders of country after country face enormous problems. The factors which have been mentioned in this chapter are cause for grave concern...and there appear to be no real answers.

Volume Three of *The Earth and the Universe*, whose contributors are from a number of prestigious universities like Yale, Harvard and Columbia, is summed up in these words about modern man: "handicapped by his inadequate conceptions, confirmed in his prison house of senses, tormented with uncertainty—beset by doubts." [104]

The space age has produced, not a utopian world, but a nightmare of technology capable of destroying the earth. The U.N. has not been able to achieve peace. Modern science has not been able to conquer hunger or disease. Rather, new and more terrifying problems have been produced.

The gloom and fear appears to be rather universal. Among other indications, *US News and World Report* articles indicate that not all is well in the Soviet camp as they attempt to march to world conquest. [105]

Stress—a twentieth century malady—takes its toll on modern man, and so the escape routes of pleasure, sport, frantic consumption of leisure time, the pursuit of sex, drugs and so on are jammed with people wanting to "forget the future." Hal Lindsey in his *The Terminal Generation* calls it "the worry epidemic." Mental illness, alcoholism and suicide are typical results. [106]

Little wonder that heart problems are the number one health concern in North America, or that current books and movies bear apocalyptic titles like: *Running Out, Apocalypse Now, Five Minutes to Midnight, World War III, The Terminal Generation, Future Shock, Armageddon* and so on.

9. FALSE CHRISTS. Jim Jones. Guyana. People's Temple.

The names are household words throughout North America and the world following the tragic mass suicide of over 900 people in November of 1978. Jones was one—admittedly the most famous but nevertheless only *one*—of the many false saviors around today.

There have been people like Father Divine, Charles Manson, and numerous lesser lights who attracted people in substantial numbers to their claims that they were christs (appointed ones) who were to usher in a new order for earth.

More recently, Allen-Michael Noonan, leader of a California cult known as The One World Family, gained notoriety through his writings (a projected twelve-volume *Everlasting Gospel*) and his claimed telepathic communication with UFOs and extraterrestrial beings.[107] Noonan's "new earth" view is admittedly "kookie"—but people do listen to him, and to many others like him.

Any number of Messiahs from the Eastern religions have come on the scene—with Guru Ji perhaps the best known during the height of his popularity as "God incarnate." Then a fat fifteen-year-old, the Guru had thousands of devotees worldwide—including the U.S.

Rev. Sun Myung Moon, the Korean "messiah," burst upon the North American scene in the mid-1970s with his claim of being Jesus—the Savior. He has attracted a large following for his Unification Church through extremely questionable methods—resulting in a great deal of controversy over this powerful, wealthy and apparently growing group.

Then there's The Way International, led by Victor Paul Wierville as founder and teacher of a cult numbering into the thousands. Though Wierville hasn't publicly claimed to be Jesus, his followers do kneel down before him and generally treat him like deity. "I worshipped Wierville without question," says one former follower. [108]

"Send Us a Man." The search for a savior
will intensify. As the apparently insoluble
problems multiply and become increasingly
severe, the inherent desire for a savior—*any*
savior—will grow.

If a man like Paul Henri Spaak, a former
Secretary General of NATO and former Prime
Minister of Belgium could say, as he was
quoted as saying in *Moody Monthly* in March
1974, "Send us a man [who can hold the
allegiance of all the people] and be he god or
devil, we will receive him," will not others echo
his sentiments? [109] The desire for such a man
will have its culmination first in the
Antichrist—but after his defeat in the Lord
Jesus Christ, Who will indeed reign.

10. WORLDWIDE PROCLAMATION OF
THE GOSPEL. The Matthew account of Christ's
answer to His disciples' questions about the
timing of His return contains what many believe
to be a most significant sign.

In Matthew 24:14, Jesus said, "And this
gospel of the kingdom shall be preached in all
the world for a witness unto all nations; and
then shall the end come."

There are several views held by prophetic
students concerning this sign. One view
suggests that before Christ will return for His
church the gospel must be proclaimed to all

227

nations. This view has proven to be a great impetus to the foreign missionary effort.

Another view holds that this global preaching will be done by a group of 144,000 Jewish evangelists sealed against harm by God to proclaim the gospel during the Tribulation period—after the church has been snatched away.

Regardless of the view held, however, (and proponents of each view can make a good case for their position) it is most significant that some *unusual* and *very major developments* are taking place right now in terms of global missionary effort.

In recent years several powerful interdenominational missions movements have sprung up. Operation Mobilization and Youth With a Mission are just two such groups, mobilizing hundreds upon hundreds of youthful missionaries who seek to go where the need for the gospel is greatest. Another group, World Literature Crusade has launched Every Home Crusades in scores of nations.

Campus Crusade for Christ, with over 10,000 staffers, is involved in dozens of nations in "Here's Life, World" campaigns designed to give the message of Christ to the entire globe within the next few years. Crusade has commissioned the production of the "Bible dramatized on film," beginning with *JESUS*, the Luke account of the Savior, which they expect to show to over 200 million Asians in

1980 alone. Their Agape movement is seeing hundreds of Christians go to other lands with the salvation message.

Many missionary denominations like the Christian and Missionary Alliance and the Southern Baptists have set goals to double or substantially increase their outreach within the next few years.

One of the most exciting developments in my opinion was the creation in 1978 of the U.S. Center of World Mission through the vision of Dr. Ralph Winter. This interdenominational effort, which envisions the establishment of sister centers of World Mission around the world, has as its stated goal the preaching of the gospel in the world's 16,500 cultures in which no Christian church currently exists. The Center, in its brief lifespan, has identified these groups and begun to enunciate studies and strategies to reach them. [110]

Another recent development arose from the Lausanne Committee on World Evangelization called by Billy Graham in the early 1970s. In June of 1980, a subsequent conference on World Evangelization was held in Pattaya, Thailand, consisting of scholars and church and mission leaders from around the world. As a result, there was an increased interest in the unreached frontiers of missions, in supporting mission agencies, and in continuing discussion of strategy for the evangelism of "hidden peoples."

229

In October of 1980, a gathering of 160 missions *executives*, both western and non-western, was set for Edinburgh, Scotland. One leader, commenting on these two very significant 1980 conferences, said:

> Thailand '80 brought its participants a long way toward understanding the realities of the world's unreached billions. This was of inestimable value, especially to church leaders around the world. An answer to the question, "How can they hear without a preacher?" was begun at Pattaya.
>
> Now that [thrust] must be completed by mission executives from 160 agencies who will gather at Edinburgh. The question "Whom shall we send?" will be addressed *for the first time in history by a significant number of African and Asian mission executives who will sit down together with Westerners*, an accomplishment only possible in a consultation of this nature" (italics mine). [111]

Whether it is realized or not, the possibility of the Word of God being preached in all the world even prior to the efforts of the 144,000 "sealed ones" is a very real one—especially when radio, gospel recordings, films, and satellite TV to even remote villages and areas with "gospel" dish receivers are taken into consideration. To many observers it's an exciting potential sign.

Yes—planet earth is running out of time. The indicators which precede the final fulfillment are piling up.

Traffic jam in the clouds? That's what some experts predict unless steps are taken to improve airports and control systems.
US News and World Report, March 10, 1980

11

Around the World in Eighty Minutes

You've probably heard the cynic's definition of jet-age travel: "Breakfast in Los Angeles; lunch in New York City; dinner in London—and baggage in Buenos Aires!"

Perhaps that's not too far off the mark. Certainly it is easily within the realm of possibility in our age of supersonic travel to have one's meals, in a single day, on several different continents. Whether the baggage usually winds up in yet another continent is a point the airlines would undoubtedly dispute!

We do live in an amazing age, characterized by many changes—but most certainly by the explosion of travel, both terrestrial *and* extraterrestrial, and by the "super" explosion of knowledge.

Both of these characteristics of our time were predicted centuries ago by the Prophet Daniel as being signs of the end of the age. Look at the prophecy as recorded in Daniel 12:4: "O Daniel, shut up the words, and seal the book even to the time of the end: many shall run to and fro, and knowledge shall be increased." Bible scholars are in almost complete agreement that this prophecy is a clear statement about the "time of the end" in which all of the events predicted throughout Daniel's writings would occur. That time will have vastly increased travel and the explosive expansion of knowledge as two of its characteristics.

How does our era shape up in regard to such a prophecy?

TRAVEL. About fifteen years ago I heard the late E. Buckhurst Pinch, a prophetic preacher from England, make a most interesting statement in an Ottawa church where he was giving a series of sermons on prophecy. He said that at the time of his grandfather's birth he had no faster or better way of getting around than Adam had—that is, his grandfather could either walk, or ride an animal, or be carried on some contrivance pulled by an animal even as Adam could have been.

But, said Mr. Pinch, in *his* own lifetime—a period of less than 70 years—mankind had

234

advanced from a state little different from Adam's to a situation in which a man could not only drive at enormous speeds, but fly, and even talk of going to the moon!

Since that comment back in the mid-60s, new modes and rates of travel have continued to be developed at an incredible rate.

Now man *has* walked on the moon and talks about space platforms, space shuttles and routine trips into space in vehicles such as the one whose U.S. prototype is expected to fly in March 1981 at a cost of $8.8 billion—according to *U.S. News & World Report*, March 10, 1980. [112]

Air travel on earth has gone supersonic—pioneered by the British French Concorde—with all of its problems and benefits. International intercontinental travel, both super- and sub-sonic, has increased astronomically in spite of rising costs. In the U.S. alone, over 300 million passengers were carried by domestic commercial airlines in 1979—an increase of 75 percent in a decade. An article in the March 10, 1980, *U.S. News & World Report* projected an increase of another 65 percent by 1990—to an annual U.S. passenger load of 500 million.

In addition to the anticipated 1980 fleet of 2,600 commercial aircraft, projections call for some 304,000 private aircraft in the U.S. by 1991—up from 193,000 in 1976. [113]

The December 3, 1979, issue of *Macleans* had

a feature on the exploding phenomenon of small plane flying in Canada entitled "Pleasure's Third Dimension." Those friendly skies are indeed becoming crowded.

But air travel isn't the only kind of travel that's been on the rise in this generation. Though its use has fallen on harder times because of the current energy situation, the automobile has nonetheless made possible widespread travel of the sort totally beyond the wildest imaginations of even our grandparents in their youth.

Travel by ocean liner and private vessels has also been a growing feature of our age—with pleasure cruises and round-the-world odysseys rather commonplace.

So widespread has travel become that a whole new "industry"—the travel agency business—has arisen, employing thousands and grossing millions. Admittedly, such travel opportunities are not evenly available among earth's people, but travel *has* increased unbelievably in the past fifty to sixty years. Ours is indeed a world of unprecedented travel—of "running to and fro."

"Around the world in eighty days" was a wild idea when the inventive Jules Verne wrote about it in the eighteenth century. But *our* generation has seen man go around the world in *less than eighty minutes*, as well as travel to the moon and back!

KNOWLEDGE. The term "knowledge explosion" has been so frequently used that it has almost become meaningless. And yet there has been, in fact, such an incredible "explosion" of knowledge in this century that its scope is beyond the comprehension of any one person.

Back in 1976, the *Toronto Globe and Mail* reported that mankind's fund of knowledge is doubling every ten years.

Scientists. Dr. John Wesley White in *World War III* says that 75 percent of all scientists who have ever lived throughout human history are alive and active today. He further states that over 35,000 scientific journals are now being published and circulated in the world; that 75 percent of the medicines in use today have been developed since World War II; that the number of books published annually is escalating at a phenomenal rate; that global illiteracy is dropping dramatically and that the number of college students is increasing on a large scale in nation after nation.[114] Dr. White also quotes the 1975 statement of Dr. Malcolm Todd, then President of the American Medical Association, who said "that about half of medical knowledge is outdated every ten years."[115]

Electronic Aids. Enhancing this scientific explosion are electronic devices that simply weren't available to previous generations. First, there's the *computer*—which is only about 30 years old. The computer of the 1980s is capable of incredible feats. We're told that a U.S. Navy "Crosstie Memory" computer can store 70 million bits of information on every square inch of its magnetic tape. A sophisticated computer can perform 60 billion transactions in one second. When Apollo XIII was lost in space, in an hour and one-half, computers worked out a way to bring it back. It's reported that it would have taken a scientist working with pencil and paper over a *million* years to figure out how to perform the same feat! [116]

Computers can fly Boeing 747s or Concorde jets, direct traffic in Tokyo, or number and keep track of every one of four billion human beings. Master catalogs for librarians, military strategy, medical data for doctors, checkups on jobless cheaters, store inventories, and many, many other applications make the computer an incredible factor in our world.

Television is another electronic marvel. By the time a child has graduated from high school, he has seen 17,000 hours of TV, giving him an impression of the world and universe that no child of a previous generation ever had. And with the advent of the satellite and the aluminum dish antenna, *global* TV to individual homes is a reality.

World-wide meetings via satellite are projected. Now, according to an April 1980 UPI release, the U.S. is planning to send mail via satellite. Under the national "electronic message system" a person inserts a letter into a post office machine. Within seconds the contents are translated into code and beamed via satellite to the post office nearest the receiver. Again, within seconds, without being seen or touched by anyone, the coded message is retranscribed into words, typed on a printer and inserted in an envelope. [117]

Microcomputers, the *laser beam* and *fiber optics* are yet other technical advances that are fuelling amazing advances in communication and the transmission of information.

David Suzuki, well-known Canadian scientist and broadcaster, was reported by *Macleans* magazine, October 1, 1979, as saying, "The most potent force affecting people's lives today is science and technology. There's no place in the world you can go without encountering science or its debris, not even the North Pole." [118]

Futurist author Alvin Toffler in his newest book *The Third Wave* divides history into three "waves": the agricultural, the industrial and a rising "Third Wave," which is driven by computer technology that threatens to transform the way most of the world lives and thinks into a world of "info-spheres," "techno-spheres," "bio-spheres" and "psycho-spheres." [119]

Without a doubt, this age is witnessing a tremendous increase in travel and knowledge.

The fulfillment of these prophecies of Daniel, just by themselves, would not be too conclusive—but when they combine with the many other signs of fulfillment which we've been considering, they become yet another important piece of the prophetic puzzle falling into place.

12

Armageddon
—The Stage is Being Set

Armageddon!

The very word is frightening—conjuring up, as it does, chilling visions of horrific battles, massive armies locked in mortal combat, with death and destruction occurring on an unprecedented, mind-boggling scale. Most people have only a vague understanding of Armageddon, but almost everyone has the impression that it is dreadful beyond words and in some way or another brings down the curtain on human affairs.

Some understand the term but relegate the concept to the realm of mere folklore, having its origin in the uninformed and superstitious past.

According to the Bible and those ''100 percent accurate'' prophets, Armageddon is for real. And it certainly appears that the stage is being set for its awesome enactment. Before looking at the evidence for such a bold statement, we must pause to recognize that predicting the imminent occurrence of

Armageddon has been a major preoccupation of various preachers and writers for the past *century*, at least.

OOPS—WE MISSED!

Dwight Wilson details this unfortunate propensity in his extremely well-documented book, *Armageddon Now*. Wilson's volume has over 1,000 footnotes involving more than 200 magazines, books, periodicals and unpublished manuscripts—many dating back to the early 1900s and before. He clearly demonstrates that the pattern of assigning appropriate biblical roles in a "soon impending" Armageddon to contemporary "good guys" and evildoers* on

---

* Inevitably, the pre-millenial camp has maintained a pro-Zionist/pro-Israel and an anti-Russian stance—with current events in either area triggering predictions of the nearness of Armageddon. Wilson also decries the fact that the pro-Jewish position often ignores the apparent injustices of the Israeli takeover of Palestine and the resultant plight of the Palestinian refugees. The refugee situation is a tragedy. However, it is a fact apparently in keeping with the prophetic foresight concerning which the comment of Paul S. Allen needs to be kept in mind. Allen said in **The Alliance Witness**, May 8, 1957, "Prophecy is history in advance, but it is not necessarily morally desirable or approved." And John Cummings, writing in **The End** in 1855 said, "God predicts in His Word what He does not applaud in His law."

the international scene actually goes back to as early as 1804! [120]

SO HERE WE GO AGAIN?

But why should it be any different now? If prophetic students have gone on record so often with wrong predictions about Armageddon in the past eight to ten decades, why should it be any different *this* time around? Why shouldn't *this* book and *this* author be considered to be just another in a long line of sincere but misguided doomsdayers?

Good questions!

I believe that the reason why we may conclude with assurance that Armageddon is now near is not because of *this* particular event or *that* event *in isolation*, which may look like a prophetic fulfillment.

Rather, it is because of the very *nature* of WHAT CAUSES Armageddon—coupled with the fact that the nature of our world today is rapidly assuming, on a global scale, the characteristics of THAT WHICH UNDERLIES Armageddon.

Let me explain.

Armageddon is the second of three great end-times wars, depicted by the chart in Fig. 2.

Armageddon then is a war instigated by wicked, rebellious, godless, deceived mankind in a futile effort to defy and defeat God. The central earthly figure in the Battle of

243

Event	Participants	Time	Reason for War	Outcome
First War Ezek. 38, 39	Russia and allies vs. Israel	Just before the Tribulation or possibly during the first part of it.	Russia desires Israel's vast mineral wealth, oil and strategic location.	God will intervene and through an earthquake in Israel plus supernatural rain and hail, 5/6 of the Russian army will be wiped out. It will take the Israelites 7 months to bury the dead and 7 years to collect and burn the debris.
Second War Armageddon Joel 3:9,12 Zech. 14:1-4 Rev. 16:13-16 Rev. 19:11-21	All Nations vs. God	At end of 7-year Tribulation period.	Flushed with power, furious over God's judgment in the Tribulation, the Antichrist will defy God, seek to destroy the nation of Israel, the 144,000 witnessing Jews, and Jerusalem.	The Lord Jesus Christ comes down from heaven and wipes out the combined armies of more than 200 million men. The bloodbath covers 185-200 miles of Israel and is "even unto the horse bridles" (Rev. 14:20). Antichrist and the false prophet are cast alive into the Lake of Fire (Rev. 19:20). Satan is bound in the bottomless pit for 1000 years (Rev. 20:1-3).
Third War Final Rebellion Rev. 20:7-10	Satan vs. God	At end of 1000-year Millenium period.	God allows Satan one more opportunity on earth to preach his deceiving message in order to give those born in the Millenium their 'Garden of Eden' choice	Satan will be successful in deceiving millions of those born during the millenial period to turn away from Christ. This horde of people will completely circle the believers and encompass Jerusalem in a state of siege. When this occurs God brings fire down from heaven killing the multi-millions in Satan's army. Satan is then cast into the Lake of Fire where the false prophet and Antichrist are, and they will be tormented day and night forever.

Fig. 2: Three End-Time Wars

244

Armageddon is the Antichrist.

Now, here are the prophetic revelations of Paul and John concerning this battle and the leader of earth's armies—the Antichrist—whom we've already considered in chapter eight.

And I saw heaven opened, and behold a white horse; and he that sat upon him was called Faithful and True, and in righteousness he doth judge and make war.

His eyes were as a flame of fire, and on his head were many crowns; and he had a name written, that no man knew, but he himself.

And he was clothed with a vesture dipped in blood: and his name is called The Word of God.

And the armies which were in heaven followed him upon white horses, clothed in fine linen, white and clean.

And out of his mouth goeth a sharp sword, that with it he should smite the nations: and he shall rule them with a rod of iron: and he treadeth the winepress of the fierceness and wrath of Almighty God.

And he hath on his vesture and on his thigh a name written, KING OF KINGS, AND LORD OF LORDS.

And I saw an angel standing in the

sun; and he cried with a loud voice, saying to all the fowls that fly in the midst of heaven, Come and gather yourselves together unto the supper of the great God;

That ye may eat the flesh of kings, and the flesh of captains, and the flesh of mighty men, and the flesh of horses, and of them that sit on them, and the flesh of all men, both free and bond, both small and great.

And I saw the beast, and the kings of the earth, and their armies, gathered together to make war against him that sat on the horse, and against his army.

And the beast was taken, and with him the false prophet that wrought miracles before him, with which he deceived them that had received the mark of the beast, and them that worshipped his image. These both were cast alive into a lake of fire burning with brimstone.

Revelation 19:11-20

PAUL'S INPUT

Now we beseech you, brethren, by the coming of our Lord Jesus Christ, and by our gathering together unto him,

That ye be not soon shaken in mind, or be troubled, neither by spirit, nor by word, nor by letter as from us, as that the day of Christ is at hand.

Let no man deceive you by any means; for that day shall not come, except there come a falling away first, and that man of sin be revealed, the son of perdition;

Who opposeth and exalteth himself above all that is called God, or that is worshipped; so that he as God sitteth in the temple of God, shewing himself that he is God.

Remember ye not, that, when I was yet with you, I told you these things?

And now ye know what withholdeth that he might be revealed in his time.

For the mystery of iniquity doth already work: only he who now letteth will let, until he be taken out of the way.

And then shall that Wicked be revealed, whom the Lord shall consume with the spirit of his mouth, and shall destroy with the brightness of his coming:

Even him, whose coming is after the working of Satan with all power and signs and lying wonders,

And with all deceivableness of unrighteousness in them that perish; because they received not the love of the truth, that they might be saved.

And for this cause God shall send

them strong delusion, that they should believe a lie:

That they all might be damned who believed not the truth, but had pleasure in unrighteousness.

II Thessalonians 2:1-12

The very clear, indisputable implication of these Scripture portions is that a Christ-rejecting mankind will be so completely deceived by "The Lie" of Satan and his counterfeit Christ, the Antichrist, that it will be thought possible for godless humanity to actually fight against God—and win!

IT'S MAN AGAINST GOD

Exactly what the scenario will be is not certain. In my judgment, this is something about which no one can be dogmatic and back up his view with Scripture.

It must be remembered that this battle is not just a conflict between *men* and *nations*—though there will be an "incidental" attack upon the Jews as God's chosen people—but rather between a *Satan-inspired world* and *Christ*. The confrontation of Armageddon is incited by the unholy trinity of Satan, the Antichrist and the false prophet. They will send dispatches to all nations ordering them to come to Palestine for this battle against the One whom they consider to be their heavenly oppressor. They will come to shake their fists in the face of God in a massive demonstration and protest against His devastating judgments. They will rattle their sabres of war in battle against God. While such insanity appears now to be inconceivable, remember the strong delusion under which they will labor, the absence of the Church, and the increased depravity of mankind. Three years or more of steady brainwashing by the Antichrist and the false prophet while experiencing the continuous wrath of God will thoroughly condition mankind to do Satan's bidding and rise up against God. In their deluded state, they will think that, with advanced missile technology and nuclear weapons, they can blow God out of His heaven.

Psalm Two describes their condition.

> Why do the heathen rage, and the people imagine a vain thing?
> The kings of the earth set themselves, and the rulers take counsel together, against the Lord, and against his anointed, saying,
> Let us break their bands asunder, and cast away their cords from us.
> He that sitteth in the heavens shall laugh: the Lord shall have them in derision.
> Then shall he speak unto them in his wrath, and vex them in his sore displeasure.

The outcome will be swift and deadly. By a word from His mouth Christ will destroy the armies of the ungodly. The Antichrist and the false prophet will be cast into the lake of fire. Satan will be bound in the abyss for a thousand years—all by Christ's mighty power.

"THE LIE"

The key thing to understand is that Satan's lie—"The Lie"—will have so taken hold of mankind that the incredible battle will be attempted. "The Lie" can be traced back to the Garden of Eden. It was first given to Eve, who believed it, as did Adam, plunging the entire human race into sin. "The Lie" with which the serpent deceived Eve was that if she and Adam ate of the forbidden fruit they would "be as gods, knowing [that is, deciding for themselves] good and evil" (Genesis 3:5). (The Hebrew word for knowing is *yada*—meaning "to ascertain.") When our original parents disobeyed God, His promised judgment for sin fell upon them. Sin and death entered the human race and the spiritual conflict of the ages was on.

The results in a society of listening to "The Lie" are that God is dethroned and human reason is deified. Man's achievements are exalted and man (in his scientific, intellectual and technological achievements) is seen to be his own savior from problems. The Word of God, divine absolutes and moral standards are all ruled out. Human reason and situational ethics are substituted.

Because the logical outcome of believing "The Lie" and ruling out God is that man is seen to be steadily evolving from a primal state toward perfection, "The Lie" promotes sensual pleasure and instant gratification, striving for a global utopia of peace and prosperity—all achieved by man *without* God.

Other aspects of "The Lie's" impact on society are that God is ruled out of public education and the state is, in fact, ultimately seen to be sovereign over everyone—including what parents can do with and for their children.

The divine concept—that government exists to enforce the absolute laws of God—is countered by "The Lie," which seeks to separate not only church and state, but God from government.

"THE LIE" HAS GONE RESPECTABLE

In 1932 *The Humanist Manifesto* was written by John Dewey and 33 other signers. It enunciates, particularly in terms of public education, the doctrine of secular humanism in which God and the supernatural are rejected to be replaced with man's reason and science. All of the aspects of "The Lie" indicated above are incorporated in *The Manifesto*, which was revised and updated in 1973. [121]

One effect of this godless philosophy was revealed in 1963, when Bible reading and prayer were declared unconstitutional in the U.S. The spiritual vacuum thus created has been filled with textbooks on immorality, rebellion to authority (including parents), the occult and other anti-biblical teachings.

Secular humanism has indeed become a religion—a fact recognized even by the Supreme Court of the United States.*

Another illustration of secular humanism's influence was to be seen when abortion was legalized in the U.S. in 1970. The laws now give the government power to decide which human beings are "persons" and which persons have the right to live.†

---

* Torcaso v. Watkins, 367 U.S. 488 (1961). The Supreme Court recognized that the first amendment grants the same protection and imposes the same limitations on the religion of secular humanism as are applicable to other religions.

Justice Clark stated in school district of Abington Township, Pa., v. Schempp, 374, U.S. 203 (1963). "The State may not establish a 'religion of secularism' in the sense of affirmatively opposing or showing hostility to religion, thus 'preferring those who believe in no religion over those who do believe.' " [122]

† A clear example of this power was the decision of the New York Court of Appeals in the Byrn Case. In 1972 this

Other examples of the growing effects of believing "The Lie" abound. Bill Gothard, in his book *Be Alert to Spiritual Danger*, documents the fact that secular humanism, while countenancing other so-called "religions," is completely intolerant of Christianity. He cites three cases.

1. A state university restricted all Christian activities on campus, while at the same time offering a course in eastern religions—complete with prayers in worship of the sun and moon.*

2. A state court brought criminal charges against parents who put their children in a Christian school rather than in a public school that was admittedly teaching the religion of secular humanism.†

---

court, the highest of that state, first found as a fact that the unborn child is a human being "upon conception." But it went on to rule that it is up to the legislature to decide which human beings are "persons" and therefore entitled to the right to live. Byrn v. New York City Health and Hospitals Corp., 31 N.Y. 2d 194, 335 NYS 2d 390, 393 (1972), Appeal Dismissed, 410 U.S. 949 (1973).[123]

* Dittman, et al v. Western Washington University, Cause No. C-79-1189-V. In United States District Court, Western District of Washington at Seattle, Washington (1979). Amicus brief filed by Center for Law and Religious Freedom.[124]

† Ohio v. Wisner, 47 Ohio St., 2d 181 (1976). The Ohio Supreme Court ruled in favor of the parents and verified the fact that secular humanism is a religion.[125]

3. A city government banned all "sex discrimination," resulting in a church being sued because it had dismissed an organist who practiced and promoted homosexual activity.*

Television's portrayal of weak fathers, dominant mothers, fractured families and the acceptance of abortion, homosexuality, and the occult, contributes to the widespread acceptance of "The Lie" throughout the western world.

In the U.S. the proposed Equal Rights Amendment would contribute to the idea that mere men and women can decide what is good and evil without regard to divine directives. The coddling of criminals and the miscarriage of justice with no concern for the rights of victims is another result.

Similar examples and illustrations of "The Lie's" effect in the Western world could be multiplied.

OUR BASE HAS BEEN ALTERED

According to Dr. Francis Schaeffer, considered to be the foremost evangelical philosopher of the day, author of more than a dozen books and originator of two epic film series, "...the

---

* Gay Rights Advocates v. First Orthodox Presbyterian Church of San Francisco, 1350 Lawton Street. 126

consensus of our society no longer rests on a Judeo-Christian base—but rather on a humanistic one...*In our time* humanism has replaced Christianity as the consensus of the West" (italics mine).[127]

Unquestionably "The Lie" is being accepted on a *global scale* today.

The French Revolution saw the Bible abolished by government decree and houses of worship closed. France is still reaping the legacy of that tragic chapter of her national history in a high degree of secular humanism. Communism and socialism with their militant anti-God, state control stance are outgrowths of "The Lie"—humanism run wild. More than half of the world today is controlled by such governments.

Add to these facts the startling global rise of satanism and satanic cults, especially in the Western world—including actual churches holding the *worship* of Satan as their declared goal, and the publishing of a *Satanic Bible*—and the outlook is clear. A major tenet of satanism is the defiance of God by men who have chosen Satan as their god.

So as never before in human history, the climate is right, the soil is fertile and the times are receptive for the rapid acceptance of "The Lie." That acceptance will lead logically to Armageddon in which a godless mankind is united to do armed conflict with God. And the growth of "The Lie" will unquestionably be accelerated tremendously when the church has been snatched away. Virtually nothing will then hold back its global acceptance.

Thus when numerous other signs (such as those mentioned throughout part three) appear against this backdrop, it is apparent that the prophetic hour is very late.

Armageddon! The stage is being set!

Very rapidly.

PART FOUR

Let's Review!

A prominent Canadian churchman and former moderator of Canada's largest Protestant church said, ''The world is dark with what seems like the sunset of our civilization.''

Certainly, as we have seen, the biblical prophets foretold such an event.

Which of their predictions may we confidently declare to have already been fulfilled, and which fulfillments are yet future?

Just how far have we come on mankind's journey through the prophetic peaks?

Let's review.

13

Checklist of Fulfilled Prophecies

Without doubt, the study of biblical prophecy (including speculation that current events indicate its imminent fullfillment) has been a compelling occupation for centuries. Within the past hundred years, however, these practices have become increasingly widespread—especially in the last decade or so.

Unfortunately, as was noted in chapter twelve, the passage of time has proven many prophetic interpreters to be wrong. Credibility has understandably suffered. And yet, it *is* clear that God *has* spoken through His prophets. The prophetic "range" sketched in chapter two *can* be clearly seen in Scripture.

Is it therefore possible to know how far we have come in our journey through those prophetic peaks? Can we be logical, sane, rational and still chart our position on the prophetic timetable?

Well, check off the following biblical prophecies—all of which are confirmed by history as being fulfilled—and then conclude *for yourself* whether or not we are, in fact, well into the "end-times."

Check	Prophesied Events	Scriptural Basis
☐	1. The division of the 12 tribes of Israel into two nations—the northern ten, Israel, and the southern two, Judah (in 931 B.C.), with both of these being carried off into captivity—Israel first (in 721 B.C.), to be lost among the nations; and Judah into an initial 70-year Babylonian captivity (in 586 B.C.). This was followed by their return to their homeland (in 525 B.C.), being conquered by Rome (in 63 B.C.); and finally ceasing to exist as a national entity as a result of their final defeat by the Romans in A.D. 70 and dispersal into all nations.	Deuteronomy 28 Isaiah 18:2 Jeremiah 9:13-16; 15:4; 18:16,17 Ezekiel 12:15,20; 22:15 Hosea 8:8; 9:17 Amos 9:8,9
☐	2. The rise and fall of	

these empires in succession: Babylon, 612-539 B.C. Medo-Persia, 539-331 B.C. Greece, 331-163 B.C. Rome, 63 B.C.-A.D. 476	Daniel 2:21-45; 7:1-28
☐ 3. The birth, life, death, resurrection and ascension of the Lord Jesus Christ. This is history's best-documented life. Jesus Christ fulfilled over 60 specific prophecies, thus indisputably demonstrating His divine nature.	Please see page 62 for a list of over 75 Scripture portions which document these facts.
☐ 4. The descent of the Holy Spirit and the birth of the Church.	Joel 2:28; Zech. 12:10; Is. 32:15; 59:12 Ezek. 39:29
☐ 5. The rebirth of the nation of Israel.	Is. 11:11; Jer.30:3;36:37; Ezek. 11:17; 20:34; 36:8; 37:1-10, 16-22; Zech. 10:10

☐ 6. The regaining of control by Israel of the city of Jerusalem (in 1967).	Luke 21:24
☐ 7. The rise to world power of a nation to the uttermost north of Israel—without question Russia (since 1945) followed by the development of a confederacy which threatens to move militarily against Israel (since the end of WW II).	Ezekiel 38
☐ 8. The formation of a ten-nation confederacy which arises out of the ancient Roman Empire (1957-1980 and onward).	Daniel 2:41-45; 7:19-28
☐ 9. The rise of an eastern power which has the capacity to field a 200 million-man army—no doubt China (since the late 1940s).	Joel 3:2; 12-14; Revelation 16:12-16
☐ 10. The move toward a global church, which is a conglomerate of many	Revelation 17

religions. (This movement has gained momentum in the decades of the 60s and 70s, coupled with the revival of the occult, on a global scale—in the decade of the 1970s).	
☐ 11. The setting of the world stage for the acceptance of a global ruler who will have the capacity to exercise complete totalitarian control over all the earth. (Deteriorating world condions, the development of the computer, the UPC, Electronic Fund Transfer and the laser are bringing these conditions to pass in the 80s.)	Daniel 2:29-44; 7:7-28; 11:21-45; Matt. 21:45; II Thes. 2:4-10; Rev. 13:1-18; 16:17; 19:11-20

Yes—indeed! We've come a long way through the peaks of prophecy foreseen and described centuries ago by those godly men of old. The fulfillment of the prophecies listed above is a matter of history which can be checked and verified by any student.

And the pace is obviously picking up.

To take a summary glance at what yet remains to be fulfilled, we turn in chapter fourteen to a consideration of the prophetic agenda still ahead of us.

14

Still on the Prophetic Agenda

So—what is left to be fulfilled from the lineup of events the prophets, Jesus Christ and the apostles foretold, and how will that come to pass upon earth?

To fully answer such a question certainly leaves one open to the possibility of being called a false (or at best, inaccurate) prophet! However, it should be clearly understood that I do not claim to be infallible, nor am I speaking as a prophet in the sense that the biblical prophets were! Neither am I dogmatic in insisting upon the *exact* chronological order or fashion in which these events will occur.

Rather, what follows is simply an attempt to establish, as accurately as possible from Scripture, a *tentative* schedule of yet-future key events. Nor is this synopsis intended to be exhaustive, but rather, a broad outline. Also, as will be understood, many of the events listed tend to overlap one another.

Furthermore, with the possible exception of

Russia's invasion of Israel and the public introduction of the one who becomes the Antichrist, I do not expect to be here upon earth for any of these occurrences—other than for the Rapture and the Millenium, of course.

I sincerely pray that none of my readers will be here either!

NOTE:

The following section of material is really "heavy." Though not exhaustive, there is still an enormous amount of information here. It is essential, however, to cover even *in brief outline* the remaining prophetic calendar. In each case, scriptural references are included to provide documentation.

If you find it too heavy, you may wish to skip to the Summary paragraphs on pages 278-281. You can always check back for the details and supportive scriptures, if you wish.

---

1. *Millions around the world disappear in the Rapture of the Church.* As we have noted throughout *Apocalypse Next*, this event is the coming of Christ to take His own (that is—all those who have been made righteous by faith in Christ, from around the world and throughout all time) to meet Him in the clouds and so to be with Him forever. This includes both those who

have died and all who are now alive. (I Thessalonians 4:14-18; I Corinthians 15:51-58; Titus 2:13). This resurrection of *dead* saints is called "the first resurrection." (John 5:25-29; Daniel 12:2; Revelation 20:5,6).

It will create quite a stir, obviously!

The rapture will be followed (in heaven) by the Judgment Seat of Christ at which believers' works will be reviewed and rewards for faithful service issued to the worthy. The marriage of Christ, the Lamb, and His Bride, the Church, will then take place.

2. *The Holy Spirit—as the "restrainer of evil" through His indwelling presence in Christ's body, the Church—is removed from the earth.* To restrain evil is *one* of the functions of the Holy Spirit. He does so, in a large measure, through born-again, righteous people who are also called "salt of the earth"—a preservative substance (II Thessalonians 2).

3. *The invasion of Israel by Russia and her confederacy occurs.* This has been considered in some detail in chapter seven. Please note that this is one event which *could* occur as early as three and one-half years before the Church is snatched away—or right at the time of the Rapture, either immediately before or after it. The reason for this flexibility in fixing the time frame is the prophecy in Ezekiel 39, which says that after Russia's defeat by God, those who dwell in Israel will burn the remains of her war machine for seven years. This would indicate

267

that it must happen seven years before the Battle of Armageddon and the immediately ensuing millenial reign of Christ (Ezekiel 38, 39).

4. *The Antichrist grasps world power.* This coming world ruler will have been introduced to the public some time prior to his power grab. He will first arise as a minor dignitary (a "little horn") in southeastern Europe, overthrow three kingdoms and become dominant over the ten-nation revived Roman Empire. Daniel calls him "the Roman Prince" (Daniel 7:24; 8:25). He will oppose Russia's reach into Israel and North Africa (Daniel 11). Then this diabolical future fuhrer will sooner or later boldly step into the power vacuum created by God's crushing victory in Israel and will take unprecedented control as the dominant power figure in the world. This will be apparently accomplished through both diplomacy and military action (Revelation 6).

5. *The Antichrist makes a seven-year pact with Israel.* Among other things this pact will involve permission for Israel to resume the ancient sacrificial system in the temple, which presupposes that a temple *will* be constructed (Daniel 9:27). This will doubtless entail a confrontation with the Arab nations. The patronage of the Antichrist and his power bloc will also stimulate Israel's rebuilding and the development of her natural resources (Ezekiel 38:8).

6. *A "World Church" unites with the Antichrist and plays a dominant role in the early stages of the Dictator's drive to global rule.* Revelation 17 indicates that this world church (described in chapter nine) will initially exercise, through its wealth and influence, a great deal of control over particularly the commerce of the ten-nation bloc. Though the papal system *may* be a part of this super-church, the latter will be comprised of numerous apostate and pagan religions. This religious entity will be responsible for the martyrdom of many who turn to Christ. A parallel spiritual development will be the salvation and sealing from harm of 144,000 Jews (Revelation 7:14) as witnesses to God, plus the appearance in Jerusalem of "two witnesses"—believed to be Moses and Elijah—who will be supernaturally preserved to declare God's truth and judgments for three and one-half years (Revelation 11:3-12; Malachi 4:5,6).

7. *Divine judgments from heaven begin to be poured out upon earth as the Tribulation begins.* This first stage of judgment is described as "the seal" judgments in Revelation 6. They are:

a) The first seal—a "white horse," as the Antichrist goes out to put down any remaining opposition (Revelation 6:2; Matthew 24:5-7).

b) The second seal—a "red horse." War and bloodshed ensue as a result of the above.

c) The third seal—a "black horse." Widespread famine results from a combination of the warfare and a divinely-appointed drought.

d) The fourth seal—a "pale horse." "Death" and "hell" pursue many, with the resultant destruction of one-fourth of the earth's population by the sword, famine, pestilence and wild beasts.

e) The fifth seal—persecution of those who do receive Christ, resulting in their martyrdom. (Note: Obviously people will be born again after the Rapture—through the evangelism of the 144,000 Jews sealed for this purpose. But, as indicated earlier, it is believed that only those who have not previously heard the gospel will come to Christ, since—according to II Thessalonians 2:10—any who have heard and have chosen to reject it before the Rapture will be sent a strong delusion *by God* so that they will believe "The Lie.")

f) The sixth seal—physical upheavals on earth and in the heavens. A great earthquake will rock the earth. (Perhaps there will also be volcanic activity since smoke and ashes will hide the sun and moon (Joel 2:30,31—suggesting shades of Mount St. Helens!). A shaking and parting of the heavens, giving the world's inhabitants a glimpse of God on His throne, will cause intense but temporary fear upon earth. Exactly what this means, or how it will happen, is not clear.

g) The seventh seal, which is a part of mid-point events and ushers in the second phase of judgment, is described below.

8. *A series of dramatic events occurs at the three and one-half year "mid-point" of the seven year [Great Tribulation] period.* These include:

a) *God orders Satan and his host of evil spiritual beings* (fallen angels and demonic forms) *to be cast out of the sphere of heaven onto earth* (Revelation 12:7-13).

b) This event is followed by *the announcement of the wrath of the Lamb*, which is the prelude to the second phase of divine judgments—symbolized by the opening of the seventh seal containing seven "trumpet" judgments (Revelation 6:17; 8:1; 9:1; 12). These seven judgments (as described in Revelation 8:69), which begin at the midpoint and carry on until the third and final phase of judgments right at the end of the seven years, are:

(1) hail, fire and blood, which consume one-third of earth's vegetation;
(2) a burning meteor, which falls into the sea and pollutes one-third of earth's oceans;
(3) the pollution of one-third of earth's fresh water sources;
(4) darkness on the earth—blotting out one-third of the light of the sun, moon and stars—perhaps the result of a thick

cloud of pollution;
(5) a five-month plague of giant locusts, described as coming from the abyss;
(6) the destructive activity of 200 million demonically inspired "horsemen"—or militia forces—with one-third of earth's population perishing as a result; and
(7) the introduction of the third, final and worst phase of divine judgment— symbolized by seven "bowls." (These will be described later.)

c) *Antichrist reveals his devilish character and diabolical goals* (Revelation 17:16-18).

(1) He destroys the false church.
(2) He breaks his agreement with Israel—halting the Jewish temple worship and substituting the world-wide worship of himself and his image which he and the false prophet have set up in the temple. This worship is enforced through the use of his mark (Daniel 9:2; I Thessalonians 2:4; Revelation 8-17).
(3) All Jews who refuse to worship the Antichrist are persecuted. Supernatural aid enables these faithful Jews to escape and be preserved in the wilderness of Edom (Matthew 24:15-24; Revelation 12:14-16).
(4) The 144,000 are apparently martyred at this point (Revelation 14) as well as

many from around the world who also refuse to take the mark of the Antichrist (Revelation 7:9-17; 13:15). The two witnesses are finally slain but will be resurrected by God after three and one-half days and will ascend visibly into heaven in full view of thousands— an event which (coupled with earthquake activity) will strike terror into the hearts of mankind (Revelation 11:7-12).

9. *Another series of horrific events leads up to the final act of the seven-year tribulation period.* These include:

a) *The seven "bowl" judgments as described in Revelation 16 begin.* Note that they are more intense judgments than those in either the "seal" or "trumpet" phases:

(1) First bowl—boils on all who worship the Beast, Antichrist (vs. 2).

(2) Second bowl—pollution of the sea, which becomes as blood and causes virtually all sea life to die (vs. 3).

(3) Third bowl—a pollution of all freshwater sources in a direct judgment for man's shedding of blood (vss. 4,5,6).

(4) Fourth bowl—intense scorching heat from the sun, resulting in massive blasphemy by mankind (vss. 8,9).

(5) Fifth bowl—darkness affecting the Antichrist's domain, causing increased

blasphemy (vss. 10,11).

(6) Sixth bowl—the drying up of the Euphrates River (whereby the "Kings of the East" can march on Palestine) as a preparation for Armageddon, and the global activity of enticing spirits from the evil trinity to lure the armies of the world to gather to Palestine for the "battle of the great day of God Almighty" (vss. 12,13,14).

(7) Seventh bowl—earth's mightiest earthquake ever erupts, causing great topographical changes to occur, destroying cities, levelling mountains and altering coastlines (vss. 17-21). This is accompanied by an awesome supernatural hail—causing men to again blaspheme God.

b) *The Battle of Armageddon explodes.*

(1) Inspired by Satan and the effects of "The Lie," armies from all nations will gather to Armageddon in Palestine to war against God. In their rage, they will especially ravage Jerusalem and destroy two-thirds of Israel's population (Revelation 16:14-16; Zechariah 12:3; 13:8,9; 14:1,2).

(2) At this point, the heavens will open and Christ will be revealed with His army of saints. He alone will wreak

vengeance and judgment upon His enemies. A 200-mile carnage will result, with special concentrations in the Valley of Megiddo and the Valley of Jehoshaphat (Revelation 13:5-17; 14:20; 16:14; 17:16,17; 19:11-15; Joel 3:10-16). The fowls of the air will be called to feast upon the carcasses of the ungodly armies (Revelation 19:17-21).

(3) The Antichrist and false prophet will be cast into the lake of fire (Revelation 19:20).

(4) Satan, the dragon, will be bound by Michael the archangel and cast into the abyss for 1,000 years (Revelation 20:1-3).

(5) All those individuals who have survived the Tribulation will be judged on the basis of their response to the gospel as proclaimed by Christ's "brethren"—the tribulation witnesses (Matthew 25:31-46). Those who have rejected will be executed in judgment to await the resurrection unto damnation at the end of the 1,000 years. Those who have responded will, with the believing remnant of Israel, enter the Millenium to re-populate the earth and serve under Christ the Messiah King and His Bride—the Church.

10. *Christ's millenial [1,000-year] reign upon*

earth begins. Establishing His earthly headquarters in Jerusalem—from which He will reign for 1,000 years—Christ will preside over a genuine utopia. Free from death, sickness, and the effects of sin such as war and the curse upon creation, mankind will enjoy a virtual Garden of Eden existence (Psalm 2:6; Isaiah 9:6,7; 11:6,7,9; 42:3,4; 65:20-25; Jeremiah 3:17; Zechariah 14:16; Romans 8:21-23; Revelation 20:4-6). Israel's borders will be extended from the Euphrates River to the River of Egypt and will be divided into twelve parallel strips, stretching east to west, one for each of the tribes (Genesis 15:18; Numbers 34; Ezekiel 48). The temple will be rebuilt and the sacrifices restored *as a teaching memorial for unborn generations to show* the truth of Christ's redemptive work (Zechariah 6:15; Ezekiel 40-49). The Feasts of the Passover and of Tabernacles will be observed (Ezekiel 45:21; Zechariah 14:16-21), though in all of this there will be no Aaronic high priest, since Christ Himself will be present to fulfill these functions.

11. *Satan's final rebellion, defeat and sentence follows the Millenium*. At the end of the 1,000 years, Satan will be loosed from the abyss for a short period, apparently to test all those born during the 1,000 years. Satan will deceive and gather from the nations all those who, though they have been born and lived under the personal reign of Christ, are unrepentant.

Acting as a great magnet which polarizes the dross of the kingdom, the rebels-in-heart, Satan will gather these (called "Gog and Magog") against Jerusalem. Here they will be struck down by fire from heaven (Revelation 20:7-9). Satan himself will then be cast forever into the lake of fire (Revelation 20:10).

12. *The Great White Throne Judgment will then occur.* At this point, the resurrection unto damnation of the wicked will take place, as all such from throughout history will be brought to the judgment bar of God—the Great White Throne—for final sentencing. The books will be opened—the Book of Life and the Book of Works—and all of them, none of whose names are written in the Book of Life, will be consigned to the lake of fire, with Satan (Revelation 20:11-15).

13. *The Kingdom is turned back to God by Christ.* After Christ's final victory and the judgment of all anti-God forces, the reclaimed, restored kingdom which had been temporarily usurped by Satan, will be turned back to God the Father. This will confirm Christ's Kingship, being a formal completion of the work assigned to Him by the Father (Isaiah 12:12; I Corinthians 15:24-28).

14. *The present heavens and earth are purged with fire and a new, eternal heaven and earth are created.* The present earth and heaven, polluted by sin and Satan's rebellion after the Millenium, will be purged by fire (II

277

Peter 3:10). Then the new eternal heaven and earth will emerge and down to this new world will descend the New Jerusalem, wherein "the Lord God Almighty will dwell with men" (Revelation 21:1-7; Revelation 22).

Thus will begin the eternal ages!

IN SUMMARY

The remaining events on the Bible's prophetic calendar for earth are these:

First will come the disappearance of a vast multitude from around the world, as the Rapture of the Church occurs.

Then the invasion of Israel by the Russian confederacy, ending in her supernatural defeat, will follow. This invasion *could* precede the Rapture. The *exact* timing cannot be dogmatically stated, inasmuch as the Bible does not make the time sequence evident.

The power vacuum thus created will be filled by the leader of the ten-nation revived Roman Empire—the Antichrist—who will collaborate with the global apostate church in the initial stages of his rule. He will make a seven-year treaty with Israel and will aid in the reconstruction of the Jewish temple and the reinstitution of the ancient sacrifices, the Temple rites.

The first phase of God's judgment upon a godless world—the seven "seal" judgments—will begin. These bring war, famine, death and physical upheavals in awesome sequence.

At the same time, 144,000 Jewish evangelists, sealed by God for worldwide witness, will begin their evangelism, supernaturally protected by God in their mission.

At the mid-point of the seven years, Satan and his hosts will be cast down to the earth from the sphere of the heavens by divine decree. The Antichrist will more fully reveal his diabolical character. He will break his agreement with Israel, stopping the Jewish worship and replacing it with his image in the temple and the order to worship him as god. All who refuse to do so—through receiving his mark in hand or forehead—will not be permitted to buy or sell. He will also at this point destroy the false church—having no more need for her. The 144,000 are now apparently martyred, as well as all who refuse the mark. All Jews who reject Antichrist's worship are also persecuted.

The second phase of God's judgments now start—as the seventh "seal" is opened to announce seven "trumpet" judgments. These are heavier and more severe, resulting in the destruction of one-third of earth's vegetation, the pollution of one-third of both the oceans and fresh water sources, awesome darkness, a five and one-half month plague of giant locusts and a destructive force of 200 million, who kill one-third of earth's population. These judgments span the last three and one-half years leading up to the final ''trumpet'' judgment, which announces the third very brief, but most intense, final phase of judgments—the ''bowl'' judgments—at the conclusion of the Tribulation.

The horrible seven ''bowl'' judgments bring boils on all who worship the Beast, total pollution of oceans and fresh water, intense heat, darkness upon the Beast's realm, the drying up of the Euphrates, and earth's mightiest earthquake, which creates enormous destruction and topographical changes.

The armies of earth are now lured, by the evil trinity, to Palestine to fight God at Armageddon.

Then Christ, with His army of saints, is revealed from heaven. The anti-God forces are destroyed by the Lord, the Antichrist and false prophet are cast into hell and Satan is bound for 1,000 years.

Christ's thousand-year millenial reign is begun with Jerusalem as capital of the earth—which enjoys an existence from which the curse and possibility of sin is removed through Christ's iron rule.

At the end of the Millenium, Satan will be loosed. He will go forth in an attempt to deceive all those born during the 1,000 years—thus giving them their personal choice between God and Satan. Incredibly, multitudes will rebel with Satan and will march on Jerusalem, where they will be consumed by fire from heaven.

Satan will be cast into the lake of fire.

The wicked dead of all ages will now be resurrected and appear before the Great White Throne for judgment and consignment to the lake of fire.

The present earth and heavens will be purged by fire; a new earth and heavens created, and the heavenly headquarters for the universe and all eternity—the New Jerusalem—will descend from heaven.

Thus will begin the eternal ages.

It must surely be obvious to any student of current events that the kind of judgments prophesied by the Apostle John to take place in the Great Tribulation may well have their foreshadowings in many present-day occurrences. Pollution, famine, drought, heat, war, earthquakes and more *are* occurring. The ridicule that even the possibility of such judgments as described in the Scriptures once evoked from skeptics has given way to an uneasy recognition that we may, in fact, *already* be seeing their forefunners!

PART FIVE

The Great Escape

"No man ever thinks that he will die...or that disaster will overtake him." Probably no more dramatic illustration of this dangerous human trait could be found than that of crusty 84-year-old Harry Truman, who refused to leave the slopes of the volcanic Mount St. Helens, saying, *"I'll be here till hell freezes over."*

A matter of days later, Harry was buried beneath tons of ash and volcanic mud.

Don't repeat his mistake of ignoring clear warnings and refusing the route out as we consider the way to get ready for the impending, awesome apocalypse.

> "The one sure lesson that history teaches us
> is that we do not learn from history."

15

The Way Out—and You!

It had been building up for weeks.

The rumbling began on March 25, 1980.
Mount St. Helens in southwestern Washington
continued sending out warning signals with
increasing intensity and frequency through all
of April and more than half of May.
Geologists indicated that, after more than 175
years of inactivity, the volcanic peak was
unquestionably going to erupt. State officials
warned people to remain well away from the
mountain and attempted to move local residents
out of the area.

One local businessman, crusty 84-year-old
Harry A. Truman (no relative to the former U.S.
President) refused to budge from his lodge on
Spirit Lake—part way up Mount St. Helens. He
became something of a celebrity, declaring that
he and his sixteen cats would survive any
eruption by holing up in a nearby mine shaft
"with a couple of bottles of whisky." Harry
maintained that since Spirit Lake was his home,

he would "spit in the eye" of the mountain, remaining there "till hell freezes over."

Numerous others—newsmen, campers, mountain climbers and outdoors lovers—ignored warnings and continued to move about, on, or near the restive volcano.

Then suddenly, at 8:35 a.m. on Sunday, May 18, Mount St. Helens erupted in the space of seconds with a blast that could be felt and heard over 200 miles away! The force of that eruption shot a column of rock and ash nine miles into the air and scattered volcanic ash and dust over six states and three provinces—in some locales to a depth of several feet—darkening the sky in a wider area of Washington state, creating floods, and sending boiling mud spilling down the ruptured mountainside. The blast was said to be equal to the most powerful nuclear explosion ever set off by man.

Over 90 persons, including Harry Truman and his cats, perished—many of them succumbing to the intense heat and/or gases emitted in the eruption.[128] The majority of the bodies could not be located and the missing persons were officially declared dead by state decree after two weeks of intensive search.

Dead—because they disregarded the warnings and underestimated the danger!

It's not the first, or worst, time in human history that people have perished in volcanic eruptions because of their failure to heed warnings. Nearly everyone is familiar with the

destruction of the city of Pompeii when
Vesuvius erupted in A.D. 79. Over 2,000
perished in that tragedy—in spite of advance
warnings that went unheeded.

In 1902, an even more incredible disregard
for a long series of very strong and clear
warnings from nature saw 29,933 die in the city
of Saint-Pierre, Martinique, when the volcanic
Mount Pelee finally erupted violently after
weeks of severe activity. [129]

Failure to respond to warnings of genuine
danger seems to be a fatal flaw in human
nature. Innumerable examples of this tragic
penchant could be cited—from both history and
current events.

That's serious enough when it involves a
matter of *physical* life or death. But it's
infinitely more disastrous when men and
women continue to roam around a restive
spiritual volcano—the eruption of which will
have eternally irrevocable and awesome
consequences.

Let me explain what I mean.

Just as there were many very obvious
warnings prior to the physical eruption of
Mount St. Helens, Mount Pelee, Vesuvius and
others, so there are many obvious warnings of
the impending end of this age. You have read
incredible things in this book in terms of the
fulfillment of prophecy. Whether or not you
fully agree with every commentary and the
viewpoint of this author, you still must

recognize that we are—without question—living in a period of astonishing prophetic fulfillment.

These events are very clear warnings that the culmination of human affairs cannot be too far removed. Now, if you consider these indications—weigh them in your mind and agree that unusual events are transpiring—BUT do nothing to ensure your personal salvation, *then you are making a far more tragic mistake than did the people who roamed around a rumbling Mount St. Helens!*

You are gambling with the eternal destiny of your never-dying soul. And you're doing so while the warning rumblings of the impending "volcano" of God's end-time judgments upon earth are rattling the very spot on which you stand.

What *should* you do to avoid the eternally fatal mistake of failing to heed the prophetic warnings God has given? How do you ensure your eternal salvation? What action should you take? The answer to those questions, which are the most important anyone could possibly face in his/her lifetime, can be summarized from the Bible in "ABC" fashion.

In order to accept the offer of God's grace and His salvation you must take the "ABC" steps of:

(1) Agree
(2) Believe, and
(3) Call

First, *agree* with God in all that He says in His Word, the Bible, about the fact that you are separated from God by your sin. Admit that you are a sinner who has broken God's righteous laws.

Agree with God that sin deserves His punishment, because He is a just, holy, *righteous* God. Admit that *you* are properly under that sentence and that you fully deserve it in all its awesomeness.

The Bible makes these facts very clear:

"For all have sinned, and come short of the glory [the standard] of God" (Romans 3:23).

"Thou [Lord] art of purer eyes than to behold evil, and canst not look on iniquity" (Habakkuk 1:13).

"There shall in no wise enter into [heaven] anything that defileth" (Revelation 21:27).

"All unrighteousness is sin" (I John 5:17).

"The wages of sin is death" (Romans 6:23).

The Bible describes three kinds of death: *physical* death (the state experienced when life leaves our bodies); *spiritual* death (spiritual separation from a holy God caused by our sin—a person can be alive physically but dead spiritually, Ephesians 2:1); and *eternal* death (the fixed state entered by the individual who dies physically while he is still dead spiritually).

It is eternal death in particular which is the

horrible result or "wages" of sin. The Lord Jesus Christ frequently described such a death as being eternal (without end) in a destiny which He called hell. He described hell as a place of judgment (Matthew 13:41); a place of everlasting fire (Matthew 18:8); a place of torment (Luke 16:24,28); a place of wailing and gnashing of teeth (Matthew 13:50); a place of remorse (Mark 9:44); of bitter memory (Luke 16:25); and a place originally prepared for the Devil and his angels (Matthew 24:41). In fact, Jesus more often warned about hell than spoke about heaven. It is not God's will or desire that *any* person should be consigned to perish in hell (II Peter 3:9), but rather that all should come to repentance.

But, as God's justice requires, "The soul that sinneth, it shall surely die" (Ezekiel 18:4).

So—agree with God, admitting that you are a sinner under God's just condemnation for that sin and that you are in need of His salvation.

SECOND: BELIEVE

Then—*believe* that God does not want you to perish eternally in the torment of hell because of your sin. Believe that God loves you—so much that He provided a way whereby He could still be a just, holy and righteous God, and yet pardon you—a sinner.

Believe that God did not just overlook sin, but that He sent His only begotten Son—the Lord

Jesus Christ—to provide salvation by personally paying the penalty for sin.

Believe that Jesus Christ (whose life, death, burial and resurrection is the best-attested fact of antiquity*) did come to earth to live, die, rise again and ascend to heaven in order to provide justification and salvation for all who trust Him.

Believe that He, and He alone, *can* save you because He has fully satisfied the just demands of God. Believe that you can't become righteous in God's sight on your own.

Believe that He *wants* to save you and that He *will* save you.

The Bible provides a solid basis for such belief:

"The Lord...is longsuffering to usward...not willing that any should perish but that all should come to repentance" (II Peter 3:9).

"For God so loved the world that He gave His only begotten son—that whosoever believeth in Him should not perish but have everlasting life" (John 3:16).

"But God commendeth His love toward us, in that while we were yet sinners, Christ died for us" (Romans 5:8).

"God hath set forth [Jesus Christ] to be a

---

* See **Evidence that Demands a Verdict, More Evidence that Demands a Verdict** and **More than a Carpenter**—all by Josh McDowell.

'payment for sin' through faith in His blood...that He might be just and the justifier of Him which believeth in Jesus" (Romans 3:25,26).

"I declare with you the gospel [the good news]...how that Christ died for our sins according to the scriptures; and that He was buried, and that He rose again the third day..." (I Corinthians 15:1-4).

"Neither is there salvation in any other [than Jesus], for there is none other name under heaven given among men whereby we must be saved" (Acts 4:12).

Jesus said, "I am the way, the truth, and the life. No man cometh unto to the Father, but by me" (John 14:6).

Jesus said, "Come unto me all ye that labor and are heavy laden and I will give you rest" (Matthew 11:28).

Jesus said, "Him that cometh to me I will in no wise cast out" (John 6:37).

Jesus said, "Behold I stand at the door [of the heart] and knock. If any man hear my voice and open the door, I will come in to him..." (Revelation 3:20).

THIRD: COME

But, *it is not enough* to agree with God, admit your need, and believe that Christ can and will save you.

You must act upon those facts.

You must repent of sin. That is, you must be sorry for your sin—sorry enough to completely turn from it and from your own efforts, or any other hope. You must *come* to Christ, calling upon *Him* for salvation, and then counting on the fact that He will do what He has promised. This means simply taking the gift of pardon and eternal life which He offers.

Merely believing *about* Jesus Christ without coming to Him makes as much sense, and is as effective, as believing that a medication can successfully treat a fatal disease, but failing to take it.

Again the Bible provides the basis for such statements:

"He that believeth on the Son is not condemned: but he that believeth not is condemned already because he hath not believed in the name of the only begotten Son of God" (John 3:18). (The word translated "believe" here means to "rest one's entire weight and trust on the object or person in which the belief is placed." It requires *action* in keeping with the intellectual assent of that "belief.")

"Whosoever shall call upon the name of the Lord shall be saved" (Romans 10:13).

"...the gift of God is eternal life through Jesus Christ our Lord" (Romans 6:23).

The logical question at this point is:

How do you come to Christ and call upon Him?

"Calling upon the Lord" is just another term for "praying," or talking to God. To talk to God is not a complicated process, dependent upon some special rituals. God invites people to approach Him, through His Son, in simple, straightforward terms. In fact, Jesus spoke with commendation of the dishonest, despised tax collector who simply prayed, "God be merciful to me—a sinner."

While the *exact* words of your prayer to God are not of vital importance since God sees and knows the attitude of your heart, the following is the kind of prayer that you could pray in calling upon God for salvation:

Dear Lord Jesus: I realize that I need You. I admit that I have sinned and that I deserve Your just, eternal punishment for that sin. But I am sorry for my sin and sincerely willing to turn from it. I believe that You died and rose again to pay sin's penalty, on my behalf. I come to You now, and open my heart to You. I ask You to come into my life, forgive me for all my sin, cleanse me from it, and make me Your child. I invite You to take control of my life and to cause me to be the kind of person that You want me to be. And I thank you for doing

this—because You have promised that
whoever calls upon You, as I have done
now, shall be saved.

If this prayer expresses the desire of your heart, I urge you to sincerely and genuinely express it to God as YOUR prayer, in the name of His Son, Jesus Christ.

Then, once you have, verbally share the fact of what you have done with someone. The Bible says that when we believe on the Lord Jesus Christ in our heart, God forgives our sins and counts us righteous, and that when we openly confess with our mouths what we have done in our hearts, God gives us *assurance* of that salvation! (Romans 10:9,10).

Follow up your decision by taking time, on a daily basis, to read and memorize God's Word (I Peter 2:2). Talk to the Lord in prayer regularly. Share with Him your desires, needs, burdens and blessings. Thank Him and praise Him—in everything (I Thessalonians 5:18).

Find a local church where the pastor and people really believe and teach the Bible—and where they are committed to obeying God in the power which He gives by His Holy Spirit.

Make a practice of regular attendance at such a church (Hebrews 10:24,25) and talk to the pastor about what the Bible teaches concerning obedience to Christ in baptism, and how to grow as a Christian. Daily invite God to control and direct your life (Ephesians 4:18).

Share your faith in Christ as often as you have opportunity—and daily anticipate the return of your Lord. Surely He must be coming soon!

And if you are someone who has come to the place of trusting Christ for salvation at some time prior to reading this book, be reminded that, as His children, God wants us to be eagerly anticipating the return of our Lord.

Jesus told His disciples, and His word comes down to us, that they were to watch for His return (Matthew 24:42). In addition, our Lord directed us to be busy serving Him until He comes (Luke 19:13).

The Apostle John adds that "every man that has this hope [the hope of Christ's return] in him, purifies himself even as He is pure" (I John 3:2). This obviously means that believers who really are anticipating the Rapture will commit themselves to a life of separation from all that defiles and a life of obedience to God, in the power which He supplies through His Holy Spirit.

And when we realize the horrific events which are to come upon this earth after the Rapture—as well as the desperate need for salvation by all who have not yet been born again—there will be strong motivation for us to share the Gospel with others as often as possible.

The Apostle Paul, near the end of his amazing life of service to the Lord—a life characterized by anticipation, even then, of

Christ's return—wrote:

> For I am now ready to be offered, and
> the time of my departure is at hand.
> I have fought a good fight, I have
> finished my course. I have kept the
> faith:
> Henceforth there is laid up for me a
> crown of righteousness, which the Lord,
> the righteous judge, shall give me at
> that day: and not to me only, but unto all
> them also that love his appearing.
>
> (II Timothy 4:6-8)

Obviously then, there is a special reward
prepared for all those who love our Lord's
appearing. May all of us who know Him live in
such a way—watching, waiting, working and
witnessing for Christ—until He comes, that it
may be our great joy to receive such a crown.

Maranatha! The Lord is coming!

If you have prayed to receive the Lord Jesus Christ as Savior during the reading of *Apocalypse Next*, I would be grateful to know of your decision and will be happy to respond with suggestions for growth in your new Christian life. Kindly address me at:

Pastor Bill
c/o Sevenoaks Alliance Church
2575 Gladwin Road,
Abbotsford, British Columbia,
Canada, V2T 3N8

Epilogue

As the enemy [Napoleon's troops] drew nearer to Moscow the attitude taken by its inhabitants in regard to their position did not become more serious, but, on the contrary, more frivolous, *as is always the case with people who see a great danger approaching*. At the approach of danger there are always two voices that speak with equal force in the heart of man: one very reasonably tells the man to consider the nature of the danger and the means of avoiding it; the other even more reasonably says that it is too painful and harassing to think of the danger, since it is not in a man's power to provide for everything and escape from the general march of events; and that it is therefore better to turn aside from the painful subject till it has come, and to think of what is pleasant. In solitude a man generally yields to the first voice; in society to the

301

second. So it was now with the
inhabitants of Moscow. It was long since
there had been so much gaiety in
Moscow as that year (Italics mine). [130]
(*War and Peace*, Leo Tolstoy)

And Jesus said to the disciples,
"...As it was in the days of Noah, so will
it be in the days of the Son of man. They
ate, they drank, they married, they were
given in marriage, until the day when
Noah entered the ark, and the flood
came and destroyed them all. Likewise
as it was in the days of Lot—they ate,
they drank, they bought, they sold, they
planted, they built, but on the day when
Lot went out from Sodom fire and
brimstone rained down from heaven and
destroyed them all—*so will it be on the
day when the Son of man is revealed.*"
(Luke 17:25-30)

Notes

Prologue

1. Isaac Asimov, *Choice of Catastrophe* (as quoted in *The Prairie Overcomer*, July-August, 1980), p. 388.

2. The First Global Conference of the Future drew 5,000 delegates from over 40 countries to Toronto, Ontario, Canada, for a five-day meeting July 20-25, 1980. *Vancouver* (B.C.) *Sun* staff reporter, Moira Farrow, in her final dispatch from the conference, July 25, 1980, quoted chairman Maurice Strong, a Canadian businessman who is the former head of the UN environment program, as saying, "The bad news is that the end of the world is coming and the good news is—not yet and not necessarily. But the decade of the '80's is going to be the most important in human history. If we don't make the right decisions, the odds of us going beyond this decade are very slim. The danger of war and the collapse of Western civilization are a very real possibility."

Chapter One

3. D. Meadows, ed., *The Limits to Growth* (Washington, D.C.: Potomac Associates, 1975), pp. 189-200.

4. Ibid., p. 28, back cover.

5. Stephen Travis, *The Jesus Hope* (Downers Grove, Ill.: Inter Varsity Press, 1974), p. 12.

6. Ibid., p. 13.

7. M. Albrecht, ed., "Welcome to the 1980's," *SCP Newsletter*, February-March 1980, p. 2.

8. Ibid., p. 3.

9. Ibid., pp. 2,3.

10. A. Peccei, Interview, *Vision Magazine*, November 1979.

11. "The Great Nuclear Debate," *Time*, July 21, 1980, p. 31.

12. "Report of the U.S. Joint Committee on Energy 1979," as reported in *Einstein: Father of the Last Days*, Oklahoma City, Southwest Radio Church, May 1979, p. 3.

13. *The Intelligence Digest*, January 1980, p. 3.

14. M. Albrecht, extrapolations of the four Club of Rome Reports and *Approaching the Decade of Shock* (Weldon and Wilson), pp. 2,3.

Chapter Two

15. *Religious News Service* release, January 23, 1980.

16. J. McDowell, Comp., *Evidence that Demands a Verdict* (San Bernadino, Ca.: Campus Crusade for Christ, 1972), p. 175.

Chapter Five

17. *Encyclopedia Britannica* (William Benton, Pub.), 1958 Edition, Vol. 13 p. 8; Vol. 17, pp. 130-136.

18. Micha Livnek and Ze'ev Meschel, "Masada," a publication of the National Parks Authority of Israel, Nov. 1965, pp. 16,17.

19. Mark Twain, as quoted from *The World's Greatest Library* in *The Beginning of the End*, T. LaHaye, ed., (Wheaton, Ill.: Tyndale House Publishers, 1972), p. 44.

20. C. Pack, ed., *Dry Bones: Two Sticks and Falling Dominoes* (Oklahoma City: Southwest Radio Church, 1974), pp. 8-41.

21. G. Keenan, "Beyond Illusions," 1979 Report to the National Committee on American Foreign Policy as reported in *The Jewish Voice*, May 1979, p. 1.

22. L. Collins, D. Lapierre, *O Jerusalem!* (New York: Pocket Books, 1973), pp. 243-435.

23. *The Beginning of the End*, pp. 45-54.

24. L. Latham, *Israel: A Secret Documentary*

(Wheaton, Ill.: Tyndale House, 1975), p. 9.

25. Ibid., p. 58.
26. Ibid., p. 12.
27. Ibid., p. 13.
28. Ibid., p. 17.
29. Ibid., p. 15.
30. Pack, pp. 8-15.

Chapter Six

31. M. Sharon, "A Very Useful Problem," *The Jerusalem Post*, International Edition, August 24, 1979, p. 10.

32. "PLO Recognition a Precondition of OPEC/European Oil Talks," *Los Angeles Times*, May 10, 1979.

33. D. Campbell, *Daniel: Decoder of Dreams* (Wheaton, Ill.: Victor Books, 1977), pp. 22-26.

34. Quoted in Hal Lindsey's *Late Great Planet Earth* (Grand Rapids, Mich.: Zondervan Publishing House), p. 85.

35. "The Rites of Passage," *Macleans*, August 6, 1979, p. 45.

Chapter Seven

36. Dr. W. Gesenius, as quoted in *The Beginning of the End*, pp. 63-64.

37. As quoted by F. Tetford in *Five Minutes to Midnight* (London & Eastborne: Victory

Press, 1971), p. 97.

38. LaHaye, pp. 66-69.

39. R. Allan, J. Hoffman, ed., *All Eyes on Israel* (Fort Worth, Tx.: Harvest Press, 1972), pp. 18-20.

40. "The Great Nuclear Debate," *Time*, July 21, 1980, p. 31.

41. *The Reader's Digest*, September 1979, pp. 84-92.

42. *Aviation Week and Space Technology*, October 29, 1979, p. 16.

43. *The Don Bell Report*, June 29, 1980.

44. *The US News and World Report*, October 30, 1979, p. 6.

45. ABC TV Network three-part documentary entitled "Democracy's Arsenal is Empty," aired May 11,12,13, 1980.

46. Pack, pp. 41-45.

47. Ibid., p. 43.

48. Ibid., p. 43.

49. Ibid., p. 44.

50. *The US News and World Report*, November 26, 1979.

51. *James Sinclair Report*, February 1980.

52. A. Solzhenitsyn, "Communism," *Time*, February 18, 1980.

53. *James Sinclair Report*, February 1980.

54. *The Los Angeles Times*, November 23, 1973; August 31, 1977; June 9, 1978; January 8, 1978; February 14, 1977; July 10, 1977; October 6, 1977; as quoted in *Today in Bible Prophecy*, September 1979.

55. TODAY (Gannet Westchester Newspapers), Tuesday, March 27, 1979, pp. 1,14.

56. Various issues of *The Jerusalem Post* from April 1979 to February 1980.

Chapter Eight

57. *Newsweek*, June 30, 1975, p. 56.

58. During a lecture on this subject at the 1980 Nakamun Family Camp, Nakamun Lake, Alberta, August 1-9, the author was briefed by Mrs. Evelyn Kwak—a camper whose position as a computer technician with Edmonton (Alberta, Canada) Telephones provides her with insights into this sort of security. She confirmed that this system is already in operation in that city through the telephone company, with major advances planned.

59. W. Wood Jr., *Cashless Society: A World Without Money* (Oklahoma City: Southwest Radio Church, 1977), p. 12.

60. Ibid., p. 5 (quoted from January 10, 1975, *Houston Chronicle*).

61. Ibid., p. 10.

62. Ibid., p. 11.

63. Ibid., pp. 12,13.

64. Ibid., p. 13.

65. "US Technology Could Mean Total Tyranny," *Associated Press* news release, August 19, 1975, *Houston Chronicle*.

66. *Canadian Business Magazine*, December

1974, p. 43.

67. Ibid., p. 45.

68. "Public Needs and Private Rights—Who is Watching You?" *The Senior Scholastics Magazine*, September 20, 1973.

69. R. Steele, *The Mark is Ready, Are You?* (College Place, Wa.: Project Research, 1978), pp. 34-65.

70. E. Gaverluk, P. Fisher, *Fiber Optics: The Eye of Antichrist* (Oklahoma City: Southwest Radio Church, 1979), pp. 14,15.

71. As quoted by H. Lindsey in *The Late Great Planet Earth*, p. 91.

72. As quoted in *Five Minutes to Midnight*, p. 73.

73. *Time* magazine report, June 14, 1967, as quoted in *The Late Great Planet Earth*, pp. 46,47.

74. Quoted by Dr. Charles Taylor in *Today in Bible Prophecy*, November 1973. p. 7.

Chapter Nine

75. H. Halley, ed., *Halley's Bible Handbook* (Chicago: H.H. Halley, 1951), pp. 82,83.

76. H. Lindsey, *There's a New World Coming* (Santa Ana, Ca.: Vision House Publishers, 1973), p. 236.

77. As quoted in *Five Minutes to Midnight*, pp. 49-52.

78. *The Los Angeles Times*, May 10, 1970, as

quoted in *The Destiny of America* (Van Nuys, Ca.: Time-Light Publishers, 1972), p. 177.

79. *The Christian Beacon*, June 11, 1970, as quoted in *The Destiny of America*, Ibid., pp. 176,177.

80. *Eternity Magazine*, March 1979, p. 68.

81. "Religion in Review," N.Y. (RNS), October 15-21, 1979.

82. A 1973 Canadian Crusade Evangelism special Newsletter.

83. *Religious News Service*, February 11, 1980.

Chapter Ten

84. C. Chant, R. Holmes, W. Koenig, eds., *Two Centuries of Warfare* (Hong Kong: Octopus Books, 1978).

85. *Associated Press* news release, April 20, 1980.

86. *The Chicago Tribune* "news map" January 15, 1980, as reproduced in *Christian Life Magazine*, May 1980, pp. 36,37.

87. J.W. White, *World War III* (Grand Rapids, Mich.: Zondervan Publishing House, 1977), pp. 46-50.

88. *Time*, September 17, 1975, p. 54.

89. *United Press International* news release, April 18, 1980.

90. *Time*, December 8, 1975, pp. 48-60.

91. *Canadian Press* news items dated January

16, 1980; March 11, 1980; April 8, 1980; April 25, 1980.

92. *Canadian Press* release, March 12, 1980.

93. *The Sunday Oregonian Parade Magazine*, September 30, 1979.

94. *The Vancouver Sun*, April 12, 1973, p. 5.

95. *United Press International* news release from Rome, Italy, February 8, 1979.

96. "Acid Rain: Scourge from the Skies," *The Reader's Digest*, June 1980, p. 49.

97. *Time*, June 21, 1971.

98. *Time*, July 29, 1980, p. 58.

99. *Enroute Magazine*, May 1979 issue, p. 20.

100. As reported in *End-Time News Digest*, July 1980 issue, pp. 6,7.

101. *The Kiplinger Washington Letter*, Vol. 57, No. 30, July 25, 1980, p. 1.

102. J. Weldon, Z. Levitt, *Encounter with UFO's* (Irvine, Ca.: Harvest House Publishers, 1975), pp. 31-43.

103. Ibid., pp. 38,39.

104. *The Earth and the Universe*, Volume Three, as quoted in *The Beginning of the End*.

105. "Hobbled Giants," *US News and World Report*, June 30, 1980, pp. 15-18.

106. H. Lindsey, *The Terminal Generation* (Old Tappan, N.J.: Fleming H. Revell, 1975), pp. 14,15.

107. J. Weldon, pp. 86-94.

108. "The Cult of The Teacher and The Way," *The Vancouver Sun*, Thursday, August 21, 1980, p. 6.

109. P.H. Spaak, quoted in *Moody Monthly*, March 1974, p. 43.

110. *Mission Frontiers*, publication of the U.S. Centre For World Mission, Vol. 2:7, July 1980, p. 405.

111. *Mission Frontiers*, Vol. 2:9, August 1980, p. 5.

Chapter Eleven

112. *US News and World Report*, March 10, 1980, p. 57.

113. Ibid., p. 61.

114. J.W. White, pp. 31-33.

115. Ibid., p. 32.

116. Ibid., p. 33.

117. *United Press International* release, April 14, 1980.

118. *Macleans*, December 3, 1979, pp. 54-57.

119. A. Toffler, *The Third Wave* (New York: Morrow, 1980), cover interview.

120. D. Wilson, *Armageddon Now* (Grand Rapids, Mich.: Baker Book House, 1977), pp. 11-14.

121. *The Humanist Manifestos I and II, 1933, 1973* (Buffalo: Prometheus Books, 1973), pp. 8-12.

122. B. Gothard, *Be Alert to Spiritual Danger* (Wheaton, Ill.: Institute in Basic Youth Conflicts, 1979), p. 12.

123. Ibid., p. 4.

124. Ibid., p. 6.
125. Ibid., p. 6.
126. Ibid., p. 6.
127. F. Schaeffer and C.E. Koop, *Whatever Happened to the Human Race?* (Old Tappan, N.J.: Fleming H. Revell, 1979), p. 21.

Chapter Fifteen

128. *Time*, May 26, 1980, p. 20.
129. *Time*, May 26, 1980, p. 25.
130. L. Tolstoy, *War and Peace*, "Great Books of the Western World" Vol. 51, p. 426.

Selected Bibliography

Albrecht, M. "Welcome to the 1980s." *SCP Newsletter*, February-March 1980.

Bethell, N. *The Palestine Triangle*. New York: G.P. Putnam & Sons, 1979.

Campbell, D. *Daniel: Decoder of Dreams*. Wheaton, Ill.: Victor Books, 1977.
Collins, L., and D. LaPierre. *O Jerusalem!* New York: Pocket Books, 1973.

Duncan H. *Secular Humanism*. Lubbock, Texas: Missionary Crusader, 1979.

Ellison, S. *Biography of a Great Planet*. Wheaton, Ill.: Tyndale House Publishers, 1975.

Gaverluk, E., D. Webber and N. Hutchings. *Why Russia Must Attack Israel Soon*. Oklahoma City: Southwest Radio Church, 1977.
Gaverluk, E. and P. Fisher. *Fiber Optics: Eye of the Antichrist*. Oklahoma City: Southwest Radio Church, 1979.

Gothard, B. *Be Alert to Spiritual Danger*. Wheaton, Ill.: Institute in Basic Youth Conflicts, 1980.

Keenan, Major-General G. "Beyond Illusions." 1979 Report to the National Committee on American Foreign Policy.

Kirban, S., ed. *The Salem Kirban Reference Bible*. Huntingdon Valley, Pa.: Salem Kirban, Inc., 1979.

LaHaye, T. *The Beginning of the End*. Wheaton, Ill.: Tyndale House Publishers, 1972.

Larson, B. *Babylon Reborn*, Carol Stream, Ill.: Creation House, 1976.

————. *Hindus, Hippies, Rock 'n Roll*. Carol Stream, Ill.: Creation House, 1972.

Latham, L. *Israel: A Secret Documentary*. Wheaton, Ill.: Tyndale House Publishers, 1975.

Lindsey, H. *The Late Great Planet Earth*. Grand Rapids: Zondervan Publishing House, 1970.

————. *The Terminal Generation*. Old Tappan, N.J.: Fleming H. Revell, 1976.

————. *There's a New World Coming*. Santa Ana, Ca.: Vision House Publishers, 1973.

McCall, T., and Z. Levitt. *Raptured!* Irvine. Ca.: Harvest House Publishers, 1975.

McDowell, J. *Evidence That Demands a Verdict*. San Bernadino, Ca.: Campus Crusade for Christ, 1972.

———. *More Evidence That Demands a Verdict*. San Bernadino, Ca.: Campus Crusade for Christ, 1975.

———. *More Than a Carpenter*. Wheaton, Ill.: Tyndale House Publishers, 1978.

Meadows, E., ed. *The Limits to Growth*. The First Report of the Club of Rome. Washington: Potomac Associates, 1972.

Mesarovic, A. and L. Pestel. *Mankind at the Turning Point*. The Second Report of the Club of Rome. New York: Signet Publishers, 1974.

Schaeffer, Francis, and C.E. Koop. *Whatever Happened to the Human Race?* Old Tappan, N.J.: Fleming H. Revell, 1979.

Solzhenitsyn, A. "Communism." *Time*, February 18, 1980.

Steele, R. *The Mark Is Ready: Are You?* College Place, Wash.: Project Research, 1978.

Tinbergen, J. *RIO: Reshaping the International Order*. New York: Signet, 1977.

Toffler, A. *The Third Wave*. New York: Morrow and Co., 1980.

Unger, M. *Beyond the Crystal Ball*. Chicago: Moody Press, 1974.

Weldon, J., and Z. Levitt. *Encounters with UFOs*. Irvine, Ca.: Harvest House Publishers, 1975.

Weldon, J., and C. Wilson. *Approaching the Decade of Shock*. San Diego: Master Books, 1978.

White, J.W. *World War III*. Grand Rapids: Zondervan Publishing House, 1977.

Wilmington, H.L. *The King Is Coming!* Wheaton, Ill.: Tyndale House Publishers, 1973.

Wilson, D. *Armageddon Now*. Grand Rapids: Baker Book House Co., 1977.

Wood, W., Jr. *Cashless Society: A World Without Money*. Alief, Texas: W.R. Wood News Interests, 1976.

APOCALYPSE NEXT...

and how you can be ready

"I'll be here till hell freezes over!"

So said crusty 84-year-old
Harry Truman, refusing to
leave the slopes of Mount St. Helens. Meanwhile,
subterranean rumblings continued and geologists
warned that the long-dormant volcano was going to
blow.

Days later, Harry Truman was buried beneath tons
of ash and volcanic mud.

Now another cataclysm is almost upon us, William R.
Goetz warns. And this one on a more terrifying,
cosmic scale than Mount St. Helens.

The evidence is here. Ancient biblical prophecies—
with a 100 percent accuracy record—demonstrate
that the culmination of human affairs cannot be too
far in the future.

You can be ready for that day.